BLACK&DECKER®

Fences
Gates & Garden Walls

Includes Newest Vinyl Fencing Styles

Creative Publishing
international

CHANHASSEN, MINNESOTA
www.creativepub.com

President/CEO: Ken Fund
Publisher: Bryan Trandem

Authors: Jerri Farris, Tim Himsel
Editors: David Griffin, Mark Johanson
Art Director: Jon Simpson
Page Layout: Kristine Mudd
Assisting Managing Editor: Tracy Stanley
Photo Editor: Julie Caruso
Lead Photographer: Steve Galvin
Photographer: Gary Sundemeyer
Scene Shop Carpenters: Randy Austin, Sean Brennan
Production Manager: Linda Halls
Cover Photo contributed by Walpole Woodworkers

Creative Publishing
international

Printed at RR Donnelley
10 9 8 7 6 5 4 3 2

FENCES, GATES & GARDEN WALLS
Created by: The Editors of Creative
Publishing international, Inc. in
cooperation with Black & Decker.
Black & Decker® is a trademark of
the Black & Decker Corporation
and is used under license.

Library of Congress Cataloging-in-Publication Data

Fences, gates & garden walls : includes new vinyl fencing styles.
    p. cm.
  Summary: "Includes 30 fence, wall and gate projects, including unique
regional styles not found in other books"--Provided by publisher.
  Includes index.
  ISBN-13: 978-1-58923-279-2 (soft cover)
  ISBN-10: 1-58923-279-8 (soft cover)
  1. Fences. 2. Gates. 3. Walls. 4. Garden structures. I. Title:
Fences, gates, and garden walls.
  TH4965.F45737 2006
  717--dc22
                              2006012067

Contents

Introduction

Boundaries represent many things to many people. A property line may mark an endpoint or a starting point, depending upon which side of the line you are one. Or, it may be a transition: a milestone on the way from Point A to Point B. How we treat our property lines is a reflection of how we see them. An open picket fence defines a boundary but can send a welcoming message too, while a tall privacy fence may signal a desire to keep the rest of the world out of our space. A low garden wall is likely there for reasons that are more aesthetic than practical in nature: perhaps you simply think it's cute. In *Fences, Gates & Garden Walls* you'll find an entire spectrum of garden wall and fencing projects that can be built to meet just about any needs and tastes.

Inside this book you will find plans, photos and hard information for building dozens of outdoor landscape projects. From classic picket fences to fanciful arbor walls made of copper tubing, you're sure to encounter a plan that appeals to you. And this new, updated version includes one of the most complete sections ever published on the fastest growing product in the work of fencing: plastic and composite fences that are virtually maintenance free once they've been installed.

A fence or a wall is incomplete, or at least ineffective, without a gate. The gate is the portion of the project that we have the most contact with and that requires the most maintenance. Gates also require higher construction standards than most fences and some walls. A gatepost also needs to be anchored more securely than a fence post, and in this book you'll find information to help you design and build a gate that meets your needs.

Whether your project is a plain chain link fence or a mortared stone wall, good planning and design are critical to your overall success. So we've included over 20 pages of useful information to help you get from a raw idea to ready-to-go.

Fences, Gates & Garden Walls

Planning & Prep

Now that you've decided to embark on a big project like a fence, wall, or gate, we know you're eager to begin digging holes and pounding nails or stacking stone. We're not out to spoil your fun, but we have to tell you this: to get the maximum enjoyment out of your efforts, you need to take a deep breath and make some plans first. You'll be time and money ahead if you determine exact property lines, have utilities marked, consider the challenges of your site and establish the goals of your project long before you gather your tools and head out to the yard.

The first real task is to define the project. Ask yourself these questions:

- What do I want to accomplish with this project?
- What do I want to avoid?
- What challenges do I face?
- What is my budget?
- How much of the work am I realistically able to do myself?
- How much maintenance am I willing to do on this structure over the next 10 years?

The answers to these questions and the information in this section will help you develop a solid plan for the location, type, style, size and building materials that make sense for the project you have in mind.

Gallery of Design Examples

Often, the best way to research ideas for fences, gates and landscape walls is simply to go for a few casual walks in various neighborhoods in your community. There you will find a living gallery of design ideas. Some may inspire and have an impact on the appearance of your yard, others will provide a cautionary message about what not to do.

On the next pages you'll see photographs of a wide range of fences, walls and gates. Each represents a solution to one or more needs. Some are mostly to provide privacy. Some are more focused on security. Others may exist primarily for the protection or containment of children or animals. But all of the examples have this in common: they work well in their environment as they uphold their more utilitarian functions.

As you analyze the design and styling of fences, walls and gates on these pages and in your neighborhood, also pay attention to the construction methods to study how fences, walls and gates are made.

Chain link fencing (above) is not regarded as the most attractive product for residential use, but it is probably the best option if you want to preserve sightlines while maintaining a barrier for pets and kids.

(above) Privacy fences are usually 4 ft. to 8 ft. tall and made of solid material, like the composite siding in the fence above. Visually, this makes privacy fences very prominent, placing extra importance on the need to make good design choices.

A stately gate (left) can transform the entry point for a yard into the sumptuous gateway to a regal retreat. When handled judiciously, nonwood materials like the wrought iron and brick in this gate provide a pleasing surprise in a neighborhood that's overrun with everyday border choices.

A gentle slope can present a very challenging engineering problem. But a fence with strong vertical lines, like the board-and-stringer fence seen here, actually benefits from the irregularity and the interest it creates.

A classic form like the white picket fence (above) creates an immediate impression on visitors and passersby. What could be more charming?

A rose arbor and luxurious foliage nearly consume this fence visually, but even though it is willing to relinquish some of the attention it is the sturdiness of the fence that allows the flowers to bloom.

A brickwork gateway adds a formal feeling and a sense of passage to a neat paver path and steps. When designing with brick, varying the colors and textures can create a very pleasing effect.

5320

Vinyl fences (technically, PVC fences) are durable and require relatively low maintenance. Initially, they were only available in blinding white, but new colors and a wider range of styles are hitting the market fast.

Stacked block walls offer privacy and security, and their hard appearance can easily be softened with climbing vines and flowers.

A loose-laid wall built of local stones makes a strong design statement in an otherwise bland garden. Garden walls can help you subdivide a large yard or garden, both practically and visually, resulting in an enhanced feeling of intimacy and a more efficient outdoor space.

Making a Plan

Making a plan begins with taking measurements in your yard. With accurate measurements you can draw a detailed scale drawing of your yard, called a site plan. Note the boundaries of your property on the plan, along with permanent structures, sidewalks, tress, shrubs and planting beds. You should focus on the areas where you'll be building, but it's important to get the whole yard into the plan. By going through this process, you may get a new perspective on how your project fits in (or doesn't fit in).

You should also physically mark your property lines as you take measurements. If you don't have a plot drawing (available from the architect, developer, contractor, or the previous homeowner) or a deed map (available from city hall, county courthouse, title company, or mortgage bank) that specifies property lines, hire a surveyor to locate and mark them. File a copy of the survey with the county as insurance against possible boundary disputes in the future.

Take overall measurements of your yard as well as measuring distances between objects in the yard as you begin to draw your site plan.

Consult your electric utility office, phone company, gas and water department, and cable television vendor for the exact locations of underground utility lines.

REGULATIONS

Before you can even begin drawing plans for your fence, wall, or gate, you need to research local building codes. Building codes will tell you if a building permit and inspection are needed for a project. Some code requirements are designed to protect public safety, while others help preserve aesthetic standards.

Codes may dictate what materials can be used, maximum heights for structures, depths for concrete footings and posts, and a setback distance—how far back a fence or wall must be from property lines, streets, or sidewalks. Setback distance is usually 6" to 12" and is especially important on a corner lot, since a structure could create a blind corner. A fence or wall may be built directly above a property line if agreed by both neighbors who share ownership of the fence.

If you find a fence, wall, or gate design that appeals to you but it does not meet local ordinances, the municipal authorities may be willing to grant a variance, which allows you to compromise the strict requirements of the code. This normally involves a formal appeal process and perhaps a public hearing.

Another thing to consider as you plan your project is the placement of any utility lines that cross your property. At no cost, utility companies will mark the exact locations and depths of buried lines so you can avoid costly and potentially life-threatening mistakes. In many areas, the law requires that you have this done before digging any holes. Even if it's not required by law in your area, it's truly necessary.

A fence, wall, or gate on or near a property line is as much a part of your neighbors' landscapes as your own. As a simple courtesy, notify your neighbors of your plans and even show them sketches; this will help to avoid strained relationships or legal disputes. You may even decide to share labor and expenses, combining resources for the full project or on key features that benefit you both.

DRAWING THE PLAN

Good plans make it possible to complete a project efficiently. Plotting fence, wall, and gate locations on paper makes it much easier to determine a realistic budget and make a materials list, and to develop a realistic work schedule. TIP: Don't start drawing onto your site plan right away. Make a number of photocopies that you can draw on, and save the original as a master copy.

Along with your site map, an elevation chart may be helpful if you have significant slope to contend with. On a copy of the site map, locate and draw the fence or wall layout. Consider how to handle obstacles like large rocks and trees or slopes. Be sure you take into account local setback regulations and other pertinent building codes.

As you begin to plot your new fence or wall, you'll need to do a little math. To determine the proper on-center spacing for fence posts, for example, you divide the length of the fence into equal intervals—6 ft. to 8 ft. spacing is typical. If your calculations produce a remainder, don't put it into one odd-sized bay. Instead, distribute the remainder equally among all the bays or between the first and last bay (unless you are installing prefab panels).

If you plan to use prefabricated fence panels, post spacing becomes more critical. If you'd like to install all your posts at once (the most efficient strategy), you'll need to add the width of the post to the length of the panel plus an extra ½" for wiggle room in your plan. But most fence panel manufacturers suggest that you add fence posts as you go so you can locate them exactly where the panels dictate they need to be.

If you're making a plan for building a wall, be sure to plan enough space around the wall itself for footings that are at least twice as wide as the wall they will support.

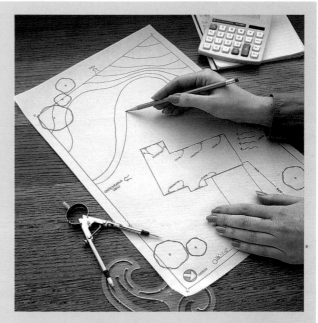

A site map is an overhead view of a fence, wall, or gate setting drawn to scale. It aids in the visualization and planning of a project. From the measurements of your yard survey, convert all actual measurements to scale measurements (if ⅛" = 1 ft., multiply actual measurements by .125). On paper, draw straight boundaries to scale.

Scribe arcs with a compass to mark triangulated points, noting the edges and corners of permanent structures, such as your house or garage. Use these points as established references to plot all the elements in the property. To finish the site map, draw contour lines to indicate slope, and mark compass directions, wind patterns, utilities, and any other pertinent information that will influence the location of your fence, wall, or gate.

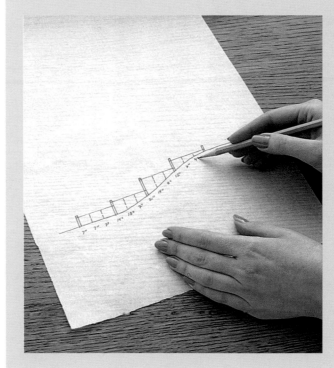

Along with your site map, make an elevation drawing of your yard if it has a significant slope. Measure the vertical drop of a slope using different sized stakes and string. Connect the string to the stakes so it is perfectly horizontal. Measure the distance between the string and ground at 2 ft. intervals along the string.

Carefully plot each corner and curve, and allow plenty of space between the footings and obstacles such as trees or low-lying areas where water may collect.

Once you've worked out the details and decided on a final layout, convert the scale dimensions from the site map to actual measurements. From this information, draw up a materials estimate, adding 10% to compensate for errors and oversights.

Solid planning and careful execution allow you to turn a sloped yard into a positive design factor when you build your fence or wall project.

Handling Slope

It's considerably easier to build a fence or garden wall when the ground is flat and level along the entire length of the proposed site line. But few landscapes are entirely flat. Hills, slight valleys, or consistent downward grades are slope issues to resolve while planning your fence. There are two common ways to handle slope: *contouring* and *stepping*.

With a contoured fence, the stringers are parallel to the ground, while the posts and siding are plumb to the earth. The top of the fence maintains a consistent height above grade, following the contours of the land. Most pre-assembled panel fences cannot be contoured, since the vertical siding members are set square to the rails. Picket

fence panels may be "racked" out of square for gentle contouring. Vinyl fence sections generally permit contouring.

Each section of a stepped fence is level across the top, forming the characteristic steps as the ground rises or falls. Stepped fences appear more structured and formal. Pre-assembled panels may be stepped to the degree their bottoms can be trimmed for the slope or additional siding (such as kick boards) can be added to conceal gaps at the tall end of the step. Stepped custom-built fences are more work than contoured fences since vertical siding boards must be trimmed to length individually and post heights may vary within a layout.

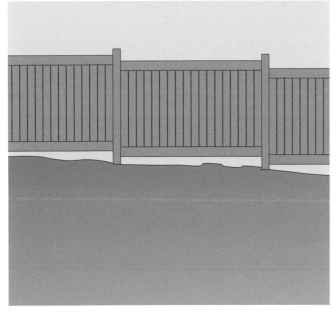

Stepped panels are horizontal, maintaining an even height between posts. A good strategy for pre-built panel systems, stepping fences is the only way to handle slope when working with prefabricated panels that cannot be trimmed or altered.

Racking a panel involves manipulating a simple fence panel by racking or twisting it out of square so the stringers follow a low slope while the siding remains vertical. Stockade and picket panels are good candidates for this trick, but the degree to which you can rack the panels is limited. If the siding is connected to stringers with more than one fastener at each joint you'll need to remove some fasteners and replace them after racking the panel.

Contouring creates a more casual, natural-looking fence. Each individual siding board is set the same distance from the ground below and allowed to extend to full height without trimming. The resulting top of the fence will mimic the ground contour.

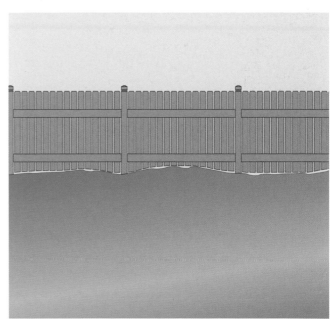

Bottom trimming creates a level fenceline with a baseline that follows the slope and contour of the land. On low slopes you can use this technique and trim the siding boards on pre-made panels that have open bottoms (in some cases you can raise the bottom stringer). Bottom trimming is best for site-built board-and-stringer fences, however.

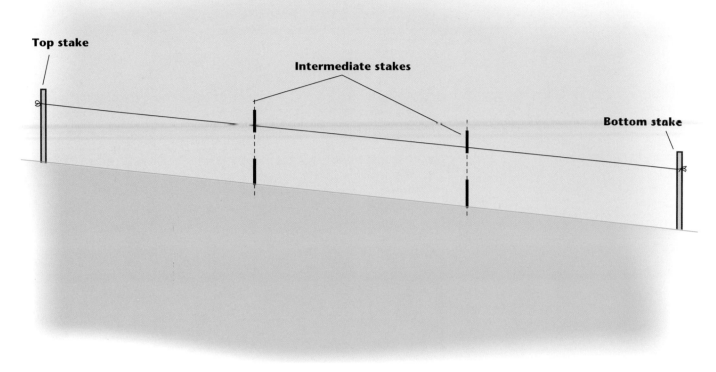

Top stake

Intermediate stakes

Bottom stake

Contoured fences can follow ground with either a regular slope or an irregular slope. Place a stake at the beginning and end of the fenceline and at each corner. Add intermediate stakes to maintain spacing when the slope changes.

CONTOURED FENCES

A contoured fence rolls along with the terrain, maintaining a consistent height above the ground as it follows the land. Picket fences and others, including vinyl, with individual siding work best for contouring. There are multiple tactics you can use to build a contoured fence. The scenario described below involves setting all your posts, Installing stringers, trimming posts to uniform height above the top stringer and then adding the picket siding.

Begin the layout by running a string between batter boards located at the ends and corners of the fenceline, adding intermediate batter boards as needed to keep the string roughly parallel with the grade. Mark the post centers at regular distances (usually 6 ft. or 8 ft.) on the string. Don't forget to allow for the posts when measuring. Drop a plumb bob at each post

mark on the string to determine posthole locations. Mark these locations with a piece of plastic pegged to the ground or by another method of your choosing.

Align, space, and set the posts. Posts for vinyl fences, some inset pre-assembled panels, and mortise and tenon rails should not be pre set. See pages 18 to 22 for more discussion on when it makes sense to set all your posts at once versus setting them as you build each individual section.

Attach the lower stringers between posts. If you are using metal fence rail brackets, bend the lower tab on each bracket to match the slope of the stringer. Each stringer should follow the slope of the ground below as closely as possible while maintaining a minimum distance between the highest point of the ground and the bottom of the stringer. This distance will vary from fence to

fence according to your design, but 12" is a good general rule.

Install all of the lower stringers and then install the upper stringers parallel to the lower ones. Make sure to maintain an even spacing between the stringers. Establish the distance from the upper stringer to the post tops and then measure this distance on each post. Draw cutting lines and trim the post tops using a circular saw and a speed square clamped to the post as a guide.

Make a spacer that's about the same width as the siding boards, with a height that matches the planned distance from the ground to the bottom of each siding board. Set the spacer beneath each board as you install it. You'll also want a spacer to set the gap between siding boards. Install the siding and add post caps.

Slope Option 2: Stepping

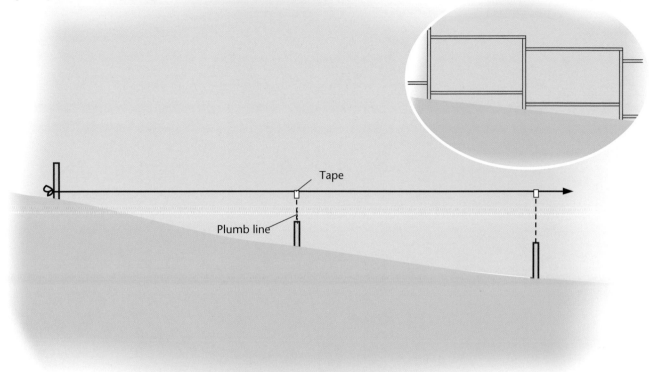

Tape

Plumb line

Stepped fences can be installed on either regular or irregular slopes. To plan the fence, run a mason's string between stakes or batter boards at the high end and the low end of the fenceline to find the total rise. Divide this amount by the number of fence sections to determine a regular rise for each fence panel. On irregular slopes, the amount of drop will vary from section to section.

STEPPED FENCES

A stepped fence retains its shape and configuration regardless of changes in slope. The effect of the stepping up or down of whole panels it to create a more formal appearance, but it also lets you avoid cutting premade fence panels. The sacrifice is that you often end up with very tall fence posts and you may need to add filler wood between panel bottoms and irregular dips in the ground.

The following stepping technique works over slopes of a consistent grade. If the grade changes much, bracket each new slope with its own stake or pair of batter boards, as in the illustration on the previous page. Treat the last post of the first run as the first post of the second run and so on.

Alternatively, step each section independently, trimming the post tops after the siding is set. The scenario below describes a flat cap

stringer, which some fences use to create a smooth top. If this is not needed on your fence, simply measure down the appropriate distances to position the inset or face-mounted stringers.

Using a mason's line and batter boards and string (or single stakes, if you know exactly where the fenceline will be), establish a level line that follows the fenceline. Measure the length of the string from end stake to end stake. This number is the run. Divide the run into equal segments that are between 72" and 96". This will give you the number of sections and posts (number of sections +1)

Measure at the lower post stake from the ground to the string and subtract from this the same measurement at the upper stake. This is your rise. Divide the rise by the number of sections you will have on the slope for the stepping measurement.

Measure and mark the post locations along the level string with permanent marker "Vs" on tape. Drop a plumb bob from each post location mark on the string. Mark the ground with a nail and a piece of bright plastic.

Set the first post at one end and the next one in line. Mark the trim line for cutting to height and run a level string from the cutting line to the next post. Measure up (or down) from the string the step size distance. Adjust marks if necessary before cutting the posts.

Repeat until you reach the end of the fenceline. Avoid creating sections that will be too tall or too short. The bottom stringer should remain at least 4" above grade.

Cut all posts and then attach stringers or panels so the distance from the tops of the posts to the stringers is consistent.

17

Use a pair of wood stakes and some mason's line to plot the rough location of your fence or wall. Then, for greater accuracy, install batter boards to plot the final location.

Laying Out Fencelines

Fence installations begin with plotting the fence line and marking post locations. Make a site map and carefully measure each post location. The more exact the posthole positions, the less likely it is that you'll need to cut stringers and siding to special sizes.

For walls, determine the outside edges of the footings along the entire site, as for a fence line. Then plot right angles to find the ends and inside edges of the footings.

Laying out a fence or wall with square corners or curves involves a little more work than for a straight fence line. The key in both instances is the same as for plotting a straight fence line: measure and mark accurately. This will ensure proper spacing between the posts and accurate dimensions for footings, which will provide strength and support for each structure.

TOOLS & MATERIALS

- Stakes & mason's string
- Line level
- Tape measure
- Plumb bob
- Circular saw
- Spring clamps
- Masking tape
- Pencil
- Spray paint
- Hand maul
- 1 × 4, 2 × 4 lumber
- Permanent marker
- Screw gun
- Screws

HOW TO LAY OUT A STRAIGHT FENCELINE

Determine your exact property lines. Plan your fence line with the locally required setback (usually 6" to 12") from the property line, unless you and your neighbor have come to another agreement. Draw a site map. It should take all aspects of your landscape into consideration, with the location of each post marked. Read "Handling Slopes" first. Referring to the site map, mark the fence line with stakes at each end or corner-post location.

Drive a pair of wood stakes a couple of feet beyond each corner or end stake. Screw a level crossboard across the stakes about 6" up from the ground on the highest end of the fence run. Draw a mason's line from the first batter board down the fenceline. Level the line with a line level and mark the height of the line against one stake of the second batter board pair. Attach a level batter board to these stakes at this height and tie the string to the corss bar so it is taut.

To mark gates. To find the on-center spacing for the gateposts, combine the width of the gate, the clearance necessary for the hinges and latch hardware, and the actual width of one post (the actual width of a 4 × 4 is 3½"). Mark the string with a "V" of masking tape to indicate the center point of each gatepost.

To mark remaining posts, refer to your site map, and then measure and mark the line post locations on the string with marks on masking tape. Remember that the marks indicate the center of the posts, not the edges.

HOW TO INSTALL BATTER BOARDS

First pair of stakes

Crossboard

Second pair of stakes

Line from first pair of stakes

Post location

1 To install batter boards, drive a pair of short wood stakes a couple of feet beyond each corner or end of the rough planned fenceline. Screw a level crossboard across one pair of stakes, about 6" up from the ground on the higher end of the fence run. Loosely tie a mason's line to the middle of the crossboard.

2 Stretch the mason's line from the first pair of batter boards to the pair of stakes at the opposite end or corner of the run. Attach a line level to the string, draw it tight against a stake and raise or lower the string until the line is level. Mark this height line on the stake and tie the string to the cross board.

3 Measure out from the starting points of the fenceline and mark post locations directly onto the layout lines using pieces of masking tape (don't forget to allow for the post widths of your posts—see tips below).

TIPS FOR SPACING LINE POSTS AND GATE POSTS

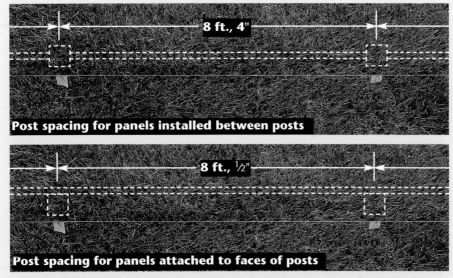

8 ft., 4"

Post spacing for panels installed between posts

8 ft., ½"

Post spacing for panels attached to faces of posts

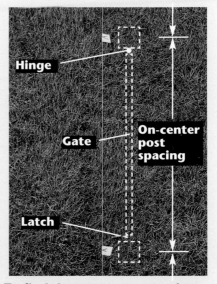

Hinge

Gate

On-center post spacing

Latch

If your fence panels will be installed between fence posts (top photo) and you are using 4 × 4" wood posts, add 4" to the length of the fence panels and use that distance as the on-center span between posts (the 4 × 4" posts are actually only 3½" wide but the extra ½" created by using the full 4" dimension will create just the right amount of "wiggle room" for the panel). If panels will be attached to the post faces, add ½" to the actual panel width to determine post spacing.

To find the on-center spacing of gateposts, add the gate width, the clearance needed for hinge and gate hardware and the actual diameter of one post.

LAYING OUT RIGHT ANGLES

If your fence or wall will enclose a square or rectangular area, or if it joins a building, you probably want the corners to form 90° angles. There are many techniques for establishing a right angle when laying out an outdoor project, but the 3-4-5-triangle method is the easiest and most reliable. It is a simple method of squaring your fence layout lines, but if you have the space use a 6-8-10 or 9-12-15 triangle. Whichever dimensions you choose, you'll find it easier to work with two tape measures to create the triangle.

HOW TO LAY OUT A RIGHT ANGLE

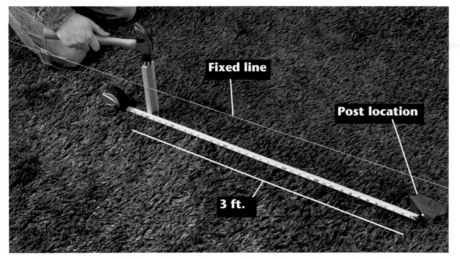

1 Drive a pair of stakes along a known fenceline and run a line that crosses the corner post location (this line should stay fixed as a reference while you square the crossing line to it). Drive a stake 3 ft. out from the corner post location, on the line you don't want to move. You will adjust the other line to establish the right angle.

2 Draw one tape measure from the post location roughly at a right angle to the fixed line. Draw the tape beyond the 4 ft. mark and lock it.

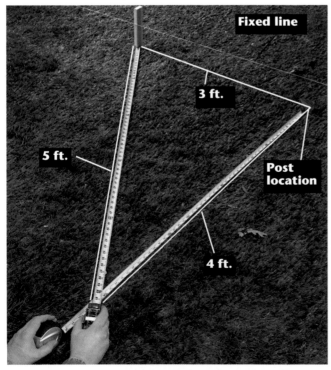

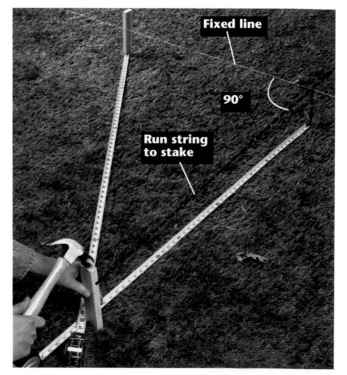

3 Angle the second tape measure from the 3-ft. stake toward the 4 ft. mark on the first tape measure. The two tapes should intersect at 5 ft and 4 ft.

4 Drive a stake at the point where the tape measure marks intersect. Run a line for this stake to another driven past the post location to establish perpendicular layout lines. The string tied to the second stake should pass directly over the post location.

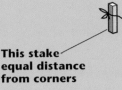

This stake equal distance from corners

Z

Y   Y

A curve in a
fenceline or a layout
line for a wall needs to be
laid out evenly to look professional. One easy way to accomplish
this is to make a crude compass by
tying a string around a can or marking
paint and tying the other end to a
wood stake, as seen in the illustration
above. The radius of the curve should
equal the distance from the compass
stake to the starting point of the
curve, so the string should be tied to
this length.

HOW TO LAY OUT A CURVE

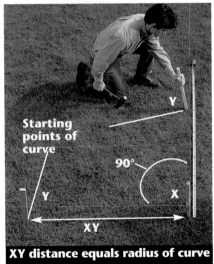

Starting points of curve

90°

Y   X

Y

XY

XY distance equals radius of curve

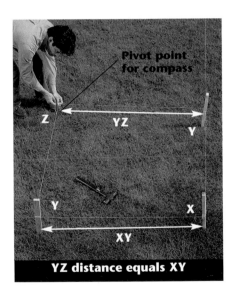

Pivot point for compass

Z   YZ   Y

Y   X

XY

YZ distance equals XY

LAYING OUT CURVES

A curved wall or fence adds interest
and appeal to any landscape. But the
curve must be plotted neatly and uni-
formly, or the planned effect will
turn into an apparent mistake.

With a few basic tools, you can
make a simple "compass" to plot the
curve symmetrically on the ground.

First, plot a right angle at the corner
of the outline, using the 3-4-5 triangle
method. Measure and drive stakes
equidistant from the outside corner

to mark the starting points for the
curve (labeled "Y" above).

Then, tie a mason's string to each
end stake, and extend the strings back
to the corner stake. Then hold them
tight at the point where they meet.
Pull the string outward at the meeting point out until the strings are
taut. Drive a stake at this point to
complete a square. This stake (labeled
"Z" above) will be the pivot point for
your string compass.

Cut a mason's string one foot
longer than the distance from the
pivot stake (Z) to a curve-starting
stake (Y). With the free end of the
string, loop around a can of landscape marking spray paint so the
distance from the pivot stake to the
can nozzle equals the distance from
the pivot to the curve starting points.
In an arc between end points, spray
paint the curve onto the ground.

Setting Posts

Even among professional landscapers you'll find widely differing practices for setting fence posts. Some take the always-overbuild approach and set every post in concrete that extends a foot past the frostline. Others prefer the impermanence, adjustability and drainage of setting posts in packed sand or gravel. Some treat the post ends before setting the posts, others don't bother. The posts may be set all at once, prior to installing the stringers and siding; or, they may be set one-at-a-time in a build-as-you-go approach. Before deciding which approach is best for your situation, it's a good idea to simply walk around your neighborhood and see how the posts for similar fences are installed, then assess which posts seem to be holding up the best.

Another area of dispute is at which point in the process posts should be cut to length (height). While there are those who advocate cutting all posts before installation and then aligning them in the ground before setting them (especially when installing chain link), the most reliable method is to trim the posts to height with a circular saw or hand saw after they are set in the ground and the concrete has dried.

Here are some additional thoughts to help you decide how to set your posts:

• The tamped earth and gravel post setting has been increasing the life span and stability of posts for thousands of years by keeping the immediate surroundings of the post dryer and firmer.

• The shallow, dish shaped concrete footing breaks all the rules, but is often the only footing that works in very loose

Taking the time to make sure posts are vertical and positioned precisely is perhaps the most important aspect of a successful fencebuilding project.

POST SPIKES

An alternative to setting posts in concrete is to use post spikes. Also called post anchors, supports, or mounting spikes, post spikes run between 24" and 30" in length, and are designed with a socket head to accommodate 4 × 4 or 6 × 6 posts. Post spikes with swivel heads help make adjustments during installation even easier.

With no holes to dig or concrete to mix, it takes little time or effort to install post spikes. To begin, put an 8"-length post into the socket head, and place the tip of the spike on the post location. Have someone help hold the spike in position as you drive it about 6" into the ground, using a sledgehammer. Check the blades of the spike for plumb with a level to make sure you are driving it in straight. Also, make sure the spike remains properly aligned and doesn't twist. Make any necessary adjustments and continue driving the spike into the ground until the base of the socket head is flush with the ground.

Cut a post to the desired fence height, and insert it into the socket head; check the post for plumb, using a level. Drive 1¼" galvanized deck screws (or the hardware screws that came with the post spike) into the pre-routed screw

holes, one on each side, of the socket head.

It is best to install the post spikes as you install the fencing. This will allow you to easily maintain the proper spacing between posts and save you from having to cut stringers and siding to special sizes.

TOOLS & MATERIALS

- Plumb bob
- Stakes
- Hand maul
- Power auger or post hole digger
- Shovel
- Coarse gravel
- Carpenter's level
- Concrete
- Mason's trowel
- Pressure-treated, cedar, or redwood 4 × 4 posts
- Scrap lengths of 2 × 4

sandy soils. Check with local fence contractors to make sure its right for your area.

•The hybrid footing helps stabilize posts in deep-freezing soils. Quick set concrete mix may be poured into the hole dry, followed by water (or not, according to local custom—soil moisture is sometimes sufficient to harden the concrete).

• Common posts are set high enough to be trimmed down to their final height. Posts with precut mortises (such as split rail fence posts) or finials need to be set to the final height in the hole.

• Dig holes two times the post thickness for sand-set or gravel-set and closer to three times the diameter if concrete-set.

The most reliably long-lasting wood posts are pressure treated with chemicals and labeled for ground contact. Species that are naturally rot resistant are unfortunately less so today than in yesteryear.

Once you've plotted your fence line with batter boards and string, mark and dig the postholes. Remove the string for the digging, but leave the batter boards in place; you will need these for aligning the posts. Ideally, your posts should be half again as deep as the above ground height of the fence or just below the frost line, whichever is deeper. At least attain the ideal with your gate post and end posts. Also set all gate and end posts in concrete.

1 Set batter boards at both ends of the fenceline. String a mason's line between the batter boards and level it. Mark post locations on the string with masking tape. according to your plan.

2 Transfer the marks from the string to the ground, using a plumb bob to pinpoint the post locations. Pin a piece of colored plastic to the ground with a nail at each post location.

Depth gauge

3 Dig post holes using a clamshell-type post-hole digger (left photo) or a rented power auger (right photo). Post-hole diggers work well for most situations, but if your holes are deeper than 30" you'll need to widen the hole at the top to operate the digger, so consider using a power auger. Make a depth gauge by tacking a board onto a 2 × 4 at the hole depth from the end of the 2 × 4. As you dig, check the depth with the gauge. If you'll be filling the post hole with concrete, widen the bottoms of the holes with your posthole digger to create bell shapes. This is especially important in states where the ground freezes.

Original position
of line

4 Reset the mason's string as a guide for aligning posts. If you want the post to be in exactly the same spot it was laid out, shift the string half the thickness of the post. Pour a 6" layer of gravel into each hole for improved drainage. Position each post in its hole.

TIP: For full concrete footings in frost-heave prone soils, cut 8"-dia. concrete forming tubes into 18" sections to collar the posts near grade level and prevent the concrete from spreading. Holes tend to flare at the top, giving concrete footings a lip that freezing ground can push against.

5 Align your post along one line or two (if it's a corner post). Brace the post on adjacent sides with boards screwed to wood stakes. Adjust to plumb in both directions, anchoring each brace to the post with screws when plumb. As you plumb the post, keep the post flush against the line. Set the remaining posts the same way.

MIXING CONCRETE

If you've never filled post holes with concrete before, you will be amazed at how much it takes to fill a hole. A 12"-dia. hole that's 36" deep will require around three cubic feet of concrete—or, about six 60-pound bags of dry mix. If you're installing 10 posts, that's 60 bags. This is yet another reason why setting posts one at a time is a good idea—you can spread out the heavy labor of mixing concrete in wheelbarrow or mortar tub. If you'll be needing more than one cubic yard (27 cubic feet) consider having ready-mix concrete trucked in. But make sure all your posts are braced and set and have at least two wheelbarrows and three workers on hand.

6 Mix concrete in a wheelbarrow and tamp into the hole with a 2 × 4 to pack the concrete as tightly as you can. Recheck the post alignment and plumb as you go, while correction is still possible. TIP: Mask the post with waxed paper near the collaring point of the concrete to keep the visible portion of the post clean. Remove the waxed paper before the concrete sets up.

TIP: Form a rounded crown of concrete with your trowel just above grade to shed water.

7 For reasonably level ground, draw a mason's string from end post to end post at the height the posts need to be cut (for custom fences, this height might be determined by your shortest post). Mark each post at the string. Carry the line around each post with a pencil and speed square.

8 Wait at least a day for the concrete to set up and then clamp a cutting guide to the posts (a speed square is perfect). Cut along the trim line on each face of each with a circular saw to trim your posts. (this is a great time to use a cordless circular saw). In most cases, you'll want to add a post cap later to cover the end grain.

Materials

When selecting building materials, consider the function of the structure as well as its appearance. Your choices will impact not only the style, but the durability, maintenance requirements, and overall cost of a project. Wood and brick are traditional favorites, but the versatility and ease of installation you get with PVC vinyl and aluminum products make them attractive options as well.

Vinyl products have become popular fence material choices. Many styles are available in a wide range of sizes, imitating just about any type of wood fence or trellis. When properly assembled, a vinyl fence is just as strong as one built from wood. But vinyl will last a lifetime with no maintenance other than an occasional bath with mild soap and water. The initial investment in vinyl is typically greater than other materials, but its durability can make it less expensive in the long run.

Ornamental metal products add a touch of elegance to a landscape. Over the years, classic wrought-iron has given way to fabricated steels and aluminum tubing that offer the same look and feel in a lighter, less expensive form. Maintenance requirements are minimal and installation is a snap.

Chain link offers premium security at a reasonable price. Made from galvanized steel, it is relatively maintenance free. Chain link offers little in terms of privacy or style, but options such as vinyl-coated mesh and color inserts are available to improve those aspects.

Copper pipe is a unique and unexpected material to use for outdoor structures. Intended for exposure to water and temperature swings, it is ideal for outdoor use. Copper materials are inexpensive and available at nearly any home center or hardware store.

Wood remains the most common building material in outdoor construction. Its versatility lends itself to just about any project, from the plain and practical to the elegant and ornate.

The most important consideration in choosing lumber is its suitability for outdoor use. Redwood and cedar are attractive, relatively soft woods with a natural resistance to moisture and insects, ideal qualities for outdoor applications. In some regions, availability may be limited, so check with local building centers before committing yourself to their use.

Pressure-treated pine is stronger and more durable than redwood or cedar, as well as more readily available and less expensive in many areas. Most home centers and lumber yards carry a wide selection of dimensional lumber as well as convenient preassembled fence panels.

Despite an outdoor rating, treated wood should have a fresh coat of stain or sealer every two years to maintain its durability and appearance. Reports about arsenic in treated lumber have raised concern among consumers, and, as a result, the lumber industry stopped manufacturing wood treated with chromated copper arsenate (CCA) for residential use as of December 31, 2003. New treatments contain no arsenic or other carcinogenic chemicals. Precautions are still in order, though. Always wear gloves, avoid breathing the sawdust, and never burn the scraps. Be sure to use corrosion-resistant metal fasteners approved for use with treated lumber.

Natural stone is one of the finest building materials you can use. It offers beautiful color and texture along with unmatched durability and elegance. But these virtues come at a price—natural stone is one of the more expensive building materials you can select, and using it can be a challenge.

Manufactured stone is often designed to resemble natural stone, but it offers greater uniformity and ease of installation. Brick and concrete block, as well as glass block, are available in a growing variety of sizes and styles, allowing you to build distinctive, reasonably priced outdoor structures.

Natural field stone

Manufactured brick, block, and glass block

Natural ashlar

27

Tools

As a homeowner, you probably already own many of the tools needed for the projects in this book. If there are tools you don't have, you can borrow from friends and neighbors, or rent the specialty tools at your local hardware store or rental center. Make sure you read over the owner's manual and operating instructions for any tools you borrow or rent. If you decide to buy new tools, invest in high-quality products whenever possible; a few extra dollars up front will cut the expense of replacing worn out or broken tools every few years. To ensure your safety and prevent damage to your tools, always use a GFCI (ground-fault circuit-interrupter) extension cord when using power tools. Because these are outdoor structures, connecting hardware, fasteners, and materials need to hold up during extreme weather conditions. The better the materials, the longer life of the structure. Any metal connecting hardware and fasteners, including nails and screws, should be made from corrosion-resistant metal that is recommended for the wood you are using. Using inappropriate hardware can weaken joints. For projects involving concrete, estimate your material needs as accurately as possible, then add 10 percent. This will compensate for any oversights and allow for waste. Also, make sure all paints, stains, and sealers are suited for exterior use. Follow the manufacturer's instructions for application.

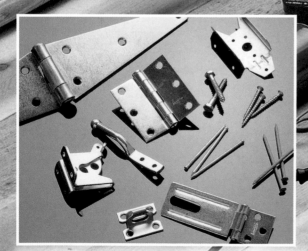

Use corrosion-resistant metal hardware and fasteners for outdoor structures: hinges, latches, fence brackets, deck screws, and nails.

BASIC TOOLS

Basic tools for building fences, walls, and gates include: shovel (1), clam shell digger (2), mason's trowel (3), propane torch (4), flux (5), solder (6), spark lighter (7), jointing tool (8), ratchet wrench (9), pliers (10), 4-ft. level (11), hammer (12), circular saw (13), chalk line (14), mason's string (15), spring clamp (16), drill (17), tape measure (18), jig saw (19), framing square (20), line level (21).

BASIC TOOLS (not shown):

In addition to these basic tools, you may need to rent tools such as a power auger, cement mixer, come-along winch, and reciprocating saw.

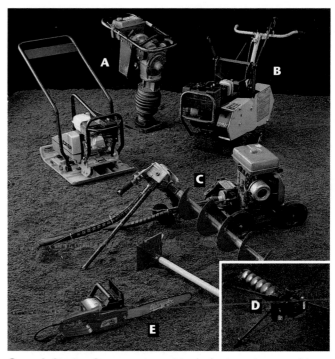

Specialty tools you can rent include: tamping machine (A), sod cutter (B), power auger (C), two-person power auger (D), chain saw (E), trencher (F).

Materials required for building outdoor structures include: paint, stain, sealer, wood glue, duct tape, cement, rebar, and gravel.

Fences

Crawling across a rolling field or guarding a suburban home, a fence defines space and creates a backdrop for the enclosed landscape. Its materials, style, shape, and colors set a tone that may even tell you something about what you'll find on the other side.

Traditional picket fences conjure up images of cottage gardens and children playing. Post-and-rail fences often surround rustic landscapes or pastures; long expanses of a white board fence can make you believe there might be horses over the next hill. Privacy fences such as board and stringer, or security fences, such as chain link, produce images of swimming pools sparkling in the sun.

If you like the idea of a fence but hesitate because you don't have time to repaint or stain over the years, a maintenance-free vinyl or composite fence might be the answer for you. They are available in many of the same styles as wood and are easy to install, with new low-maintenance options hitting the market every year.

You might be surprised at how easily you can add some pizazz to a plain fence. Try building a shadow box bay, adding a framed opening, or building a display shelf.

IN THIS CHAPTER:

Types of Fences

Choosing a fence for your yard entails more than deciding what you like best. Different types of fences serve different purposes—start by deciding what you want the fence to accomplish.

To select a specific style, decide on your main priority: privacy when working in your garden, keeping the kids or pets in a safe, enclosed area, security for a backyard pool, or the addition of a design element to your landscape. Depending on its purpose, such as surrounding a pool, local building codes may dictate some of your choices, so be sure to review the regulations before deciding on a type or style of fence.

Other considerations may include screening out an unsightly view, blocking wind and noise, or protecting gardens or flower beds. Keep in mind that an open or partially-open fence is a more effective windbreak than a solid fence. Wind simply vaults over a solid fence. An open design diffuses the wind current and protects a larger area behind the fence from the force of the wind.

Consider, too, how you want your fence to relate to your site: as an extension of the house, a part of the garden or yard, or a link between the two. Note the scale of your property and gradation. A fence that is too tall may look out of place on a small lot.

Stick-built Wood Fences
- Board & Stringer (below)
- Classic Picket Fence

Prefabricated Wood Fence Panels
• Privacy Panels
• Ornamental Picket Sections

Post-and-Rail Fences
• Split Rail   • Capped Split Rail
• Virginia Rail (above)

Prefabricated Wood Fence Panels
• Privacy Panels (above)
• Ornamental Picket Sections

Nonwood Fence Panels
• White Vinyl (PVC)
• Wood-tone Composite

Ornamental Metal Fences
• Wrought Iron Style (Above)

Chain Link Fences
• Standard (Above)
• Chain Fabric on Wood

Board & Stringer Fences

If you want a high-quality, well-built wood fence, a board and stringer fence may be the best answer. This fence style is constructed from a simple frame with at least two rails, called stringers, that run parallel to the ground between posts to form the framework. Vertical boards, called siding or infill, are attached to the framework to create the fence.

A board and stringer fence is well-suited for yards of almost any contour. Consult the section on handling slope for instructions on how to adapt fences to a sloped yard. We used pre-cut dog-eared cedar fenceboards for the siding in this project, but these construction methods can be used with many siding types and patterns. For additional ideas, spend a little time looking at magazines and driving through your favorite neighborhoods—you're certain to find a siding style that appeals to you and suits your property.

See the previous chapter for information on laying out your project and installing fence posts.

HOW TO BUILD A BOARD & STRINGER FENCE

Trim the Posts & Add the Top Stringers

Lay out the fence line and install the posts. Let the concrete cure for at least two days.

For level ground, measure up from the ground to a point 12" below the planned fence height at the end posts. Snap a chalkline across all posts at this height. Trim the posts to height with a circular saw.

Individually mark and cut 2 × 4 top stringers to span from post-center to post-center. Stringers at the end posts and gateposts should cover the full width of these posts. Miter stringers at corner posts.

Place the stringers flat on top of the posts, centering the joints except at the end posts and gateposts. Attach with 3" deck screws.

Install the Remaining Stringers

Measure down from the top rail to set your other rail or rails at a consistent distance (typically, about 2 feet) apart. Measure up from the ground to the lower rail bottoms, which should clear the ground by at least four inches.

Dog-eared siding

Stringers

Gate hardware

2" fence brackets

4 × 4 post

GATE POST LAYOUT

Hinge

Footing

On-center post spacing

Gate

Gravel

Latch

TOOLS & MATERIALS

- Tools & materials for setting posts
- Tape measure
- Chalk line
- Line level
- dip bucket with wood preservative
- Paintbrush
- Circular saw
- Hammer
- Drill
- Level
- Wood sealer/ protectant or paint
- Prefabricated gate & hardware

- Pressure-treated, cedar, or redwood lumber:4 × 4s, 2 × 4s, 1 × 6s,
- Hot-dipped (H.D.) galvanized 2 × 4 fence brackets
- H. D. galvanized nails
- H.D. galvanized deck screws
- H.D. galvanized fence bracket nails
- 2" galvanized deck screws
- ⅛" piece of scrap wood
- Wood scraps for shims

At each mark, drive galvanized joist hanger nails to secure a 2 × 4 fence bracket to the inside face of the post, flush with the outside edge.

Position a 2 × 4 between each pair of brackets. Hold or tack the board against the posts, and scribe the back side along the edges of the posts.

Cut the stringers ¼" shorter than marked, so they will slide into the brackets easily. Nail the stringers in place using joist hanger nails.

Attach the Siding

Beginning at an end post, measure from the ground to the top edge of the top stringer and add 8½". Cut a 1 × 6 to this length.

Position the 1 × 6 so that its top extends 10½" above the top stringer, leaving a 2" gap at the bottom. Make sure the siding board is plumb, then attach it to the post and rails with pairs of 2" galvanized deck screws.

Measure, cut, and attach the remaining siding to the stringers, using the same procedure. Leave a gap of at least ⅛" between boards, using pieces of scrap wood for spacers. If necessary, rip boards at the edges to make them fit.

If you're installing a gate, attach gate hinges to the hinge side of the gate frame. Shim the gate into position between the gate posts. Drill pilot holes and attach the hinges to the gate post. Attach the latch hardware to the fence and to the gate. Open and close the gate to make sure the latch works correctly. Make adjustments if necessary.

Paint or stain the fence and gate, or coat with clear sealer.

1 Trim the posts, and attach the cut stringers on top of the posts with 3" galvanized deck screws. Stringer joints should be centered on the posts.

2 Attach fence brackets to the inside faces of the posts. Set the stringers in the brackets, then fasten the stringers with nails or deck screws.

3 Measure and cut the siding boards to length. Attach the boards to the framework with 1⅝" deck screws or narrow-crown staples and a pneumatic stapler, spacing them at least ⅛" apart. Use spacers to ensure consistent gaps.

Picket Fences

For generations, the idyllic dream home has been a vine-covered cottage surrounded by a white picket fence. These days, the diversity in designs and styles of this classic American fence have expanded the range of possibilities, making the picket fence easy to adapt to any home, from an elaborate Victorian "Painted Lady" to a modest rambler.

The charm of a picket fence lies in its open and inviting appearance. The repetitive structure and spacing create a pleasing rhythm that welcomes family and friends while maintaining a fixed property division.

Traditionally, picket fences are 36" to 48" tall. The version shown here is 48" tall, with posts spaced 96" apart on-center and pickets spaced 1¾" apart. It's important that the spacing appear consistent. Using a jig or spacer to set the pickets simplifies that process.

Picket fences are usually white; however, matching your house's trim color or stain can be an eye-catching alternative. Painting the fence black or another dark color makes it look more substantial. If you prime and paint all the materials before construction, apply the second coat of paint after the fence is completed to cover any marks, smudges, and nail or screw heads.

There are a number of picket styles to choose from. Most building centers carry a variety, or you can design your own by simply creating a template. If you need a large quantity of pickets or want to use an intricate design, contact a cabinet shop in your area about making them for you—the time saved may be worth the added expense.

HOW TO BUILD A PICKET FENCE

Prepare the Materials

Lay out the fence line with batter boards and mason's string. Space the post locations every 96" on-center.

Count the 4 × 4 posts and estimate the number of pickets you'll need to complete the project. Since it's likely you'll make a cutting error or two, add 10 percent to your total.

If you're creating your own pickets, cut 1 × 4s to length. (Our design calls for 46" pickets.) Trim simple pointed pickets with a power miter saw. For more elaborate designs like the one shown here, make a template, then use a jig saw (or other appropriate cutting tool) to cut the pickets. Apply the first coat of primer and paint, stain, or sealer to all surfaces of each picket.

Set the Posts

Set the posts. Allow the concrete footings to dry for two days. Measure up 48" from ground level at each post and mark cutting lines. Trim the posts along the cutting lines, using a circular saw, reciprocating saw or handsaw.

Build the Framework

Mark a line 6" down from the top of each post to indicate the upper stringer position, and mark another line 36½" from each post top to indicate the lower stringer.

At the upper stringer marks on the first two posts, clamp an 8-ft. long 2 × 4 that's oriented so the top edge of the 2 × 4 is flush with the mark. Scribe the post outline on the back of the stringer at each end. Remove and cut the upper stringer to length. Position the upper stringer between the two posts, set back ¾"

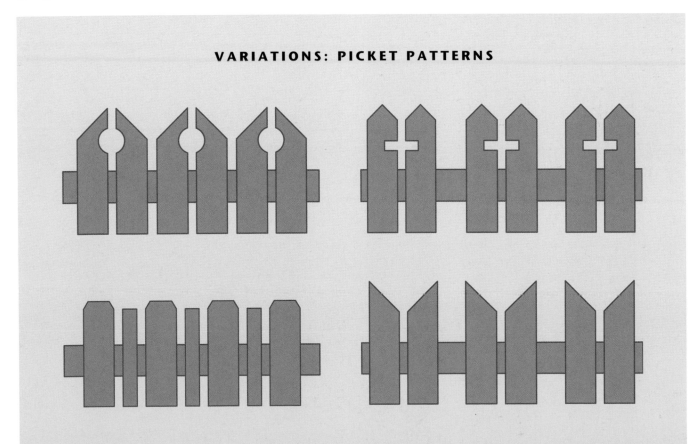

VARIATIONS: PICKET PATTERNS

1 Mark the fence line and calculate the number of posts and pickets required. Cut pickets, using a template and a jig saw.

2 Set the posts, then trim them so the tops are 48" above the ground. You can use a reciprocating saw, but a circular saw or hand saw creates less vibration and makes a smoother cut.

3 Mark the stringer position on the posts, then scribe and cut the stringer to length.

4 Toenail the stringer to the posts with 16d galvanized finish nails (inset). Drill pilot holes for the nails to prevent splitting.

from the faces of the posts. Toe-nail the stringer into place with 16d corrosion-resistant nails. Install the remaining upper and lower stringers.

Install the Pickets

To compensate for slope or shorter sections, calculate the picket spacing and decide on the number of pickets you want between posts. Multiply that number by the width of a single picket. This is the total width of pickets between the posts. Subtract that number from the total distance between the posts. The remainder equals the unoccupied space. Divide that number by the number of pickets, minus 1 (the number of spaces that will exist between the posts).

The resulting number equals the picket spacing.

To make a spacing jig, rip a 1 × 4 to the spacing size—1¾" in this project. Attach a scrap of wood to one end of the board as a cleat.

Draw a reference mark on each picket, 6" down from the peak. Place a picket flat against the stringers and slide it flush against the post. Adjust the picket until the reference line is flush with the top edge of the upper stringer. Drill pilot holes and attach the pickct, using 1½" deck screws. Hang the jig on the upper stringer and hold it flush against the attached picket. Position a new picket flush against the jig and attach it. Reposition the jig and continue along the fence line.

Apply Finishing Details

Attach fence post finials for detail. Use a straight-edge to draw lines from corner to corner on the top of the post to determine the center. Drill a pilot hole where the lines intersect and attach a finial or post cap at the center of each post. On painted fences, apply the second coat of paint.

PICKET SPACING EXAMPLE:

18 (pickets) x 3½" (picket width) = 63" (total width of run of pickets).

92½" (space between posts) − 63" = 29½" (unoccupied space).

29½" ÷ 17 (18 pickets − 1) = 1¾" (space between pickets).

Note: Not all calculations will work out evenly. If your figures come out uneven, make slight adjustments across the entire fence section.

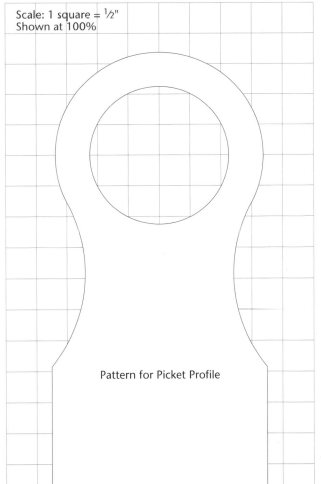

Scale: 1 square = ½"
Shown at 100%

Pattern for Picket Profile

5 Calculate the picket spacing and make a spacing jig. Position the first picket and secure it with 1½" long corrosion-resistant deck screws. Using the spacing jig, position and install the remaining pickets.

6 Determine the centers of the post tops, drill pilot holes, and attach fence post finials or caps.

39

Wood Panel Fences

Prefabricated fence panels take much of the work out of putting up a fence, and (surprisingly) using them is often less expensive than building a board-and-stringer fence from scratch. They are best suited for relatively flat yards, but may be stepped down on slopes that aren't too steep.

Fence panels come in many styles, ranging from privacy to picket. Most tend to be built lighter than fences you'd make from scratch, with thinner wood for the stringers and siding. When shopping for panels, compare quality and heft of lumber and fasteners as well as cost.

Purchase panels, gate hardware, and gate (if you're not building yours) before setting and trimming your posts. Determine also if panels can be trimmed or reproduced from scratch for short sections.

The most exacting task when building a panel fence involves insetting the panels between the posts. This requires that pre-set posts be precisely spaced and perfectly plumb. In our inset panel sequence (page 43), we set one post at a time as the fence was built, so the attached panel position can determine the spacing, not the pre-set posts.

An alternative installation to setting panels between posts is to attach them to the post faces. Face mounted panels are more forgiving of preset posts, since the attachment point of stringers doesn't need to be dead center on the posts.

Wood fence panels usually are constructed in either 6' or 8' lengths. Cedar and pressure-treated pine are the most common wood types used in making fence panels, although you may also find redwood in some areas. Generally, the cedar panels cost half-again to twice as much for similar styles.

When selecting wood fence panels, inspect every board in each panel carefully (and be sure to check both sides of the panel). These products are fairly susceptible to damage during shipping.

Building with wood fence panels is a great time saver and allows you to create a more elaborate fence than you may be able to building the parts yourself from scratch.

VARIATIONS: BOARD PATTERNS

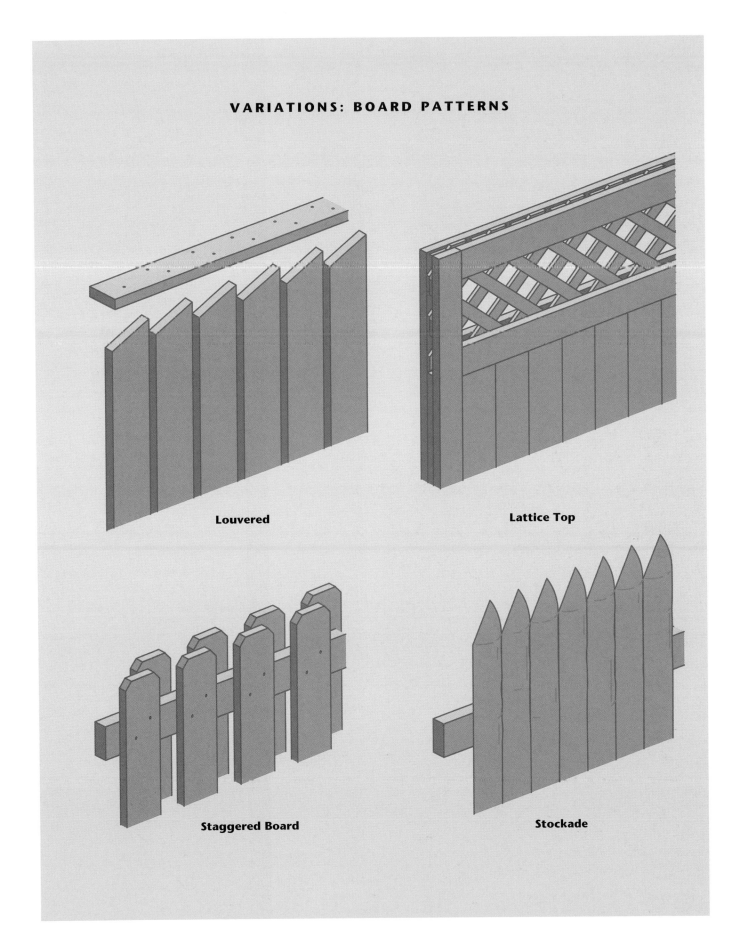

Louvered

Lattice Top

Staggered Board

Stockade

WOOD FENCE PANELS

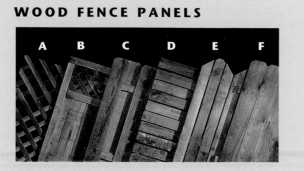

A B C D E F

Preassembled fence panels are an attractive, time-saving option when building a fence. The entire panel is attached to the posts, eliminating the need to individually cut and attach stringers.

Some popular styles of wood panels include:

A. Lattice panels
B. Solid panels
   with lattice tops
C. Staggered board
D. Horizontal board
E. Modified picket
F. Dog-eared board

Flatten tab when installling hanger

Bend tab up after panel is installed

Metal fence panel hangers make quick work of hanging panels and offer a slight amount of wiggle room if the panels is up to ½" narrower than the space between posts. With some panel styles, the best tactic is to flatten the lower tab after attaching it to the post and then bend it up or down against the panel frame once the panel is in place.

OPTION: Setting all of the posts in concrete at one time and then installing the panels after the concrete sets has advantages as well as disadvantages. On the plus side, this approach lets you pour all of the concrete at the same time and provides good access so you can make absolutely certain the posts are level and plumb. On the downside, if the post spacing is off even a little bit, you'll need to trim the panel (which can be tricky) or attach a shim to the post or the panel frame (also tricky). This is why most panel manufacturers recommend installing the posts as you go.

TIP: With some fence panels types, it's possible to disassemble the frame, trim it down to width (3 ft. to 4 ft.) and then reassemble it into a gate that matches the panels. Some manufacturers offer prefabricated gates that match their panel styles.

HOW TO BUILD A WOOD PANEL FENCE

Dig Holes, Brace End Post

Lay out the fence line and mark the post hole locations. Space the holes to fit the panels you've purchased, adding the actual post diameter (3½" for 4" nominal posts) plus ¼" for brackets to the length of a panel. Measure spacing for stepped fences on a level line, not along the slope.

Dig the first two holes of a run and tamp gravel into the hole bottoms for drainage. Position, plumb and stake the end post, adding a forming tube at the top of the hole if needed. Set your bracing so it won't interfere with the first panel. If you're renting an auger, you may want to dig all your holes at once, otherwise, digging as you go leaves room for spacing adjustment if needed. Use a stake to hold your alignment line out of the way while digging.

Fill your first post hole with concrete and tamp it into the post hole with the end of a 2 × 4.

TOOLS & MATERIALS

- Pressure-treated, cedar, or redwood 4 × 4 posts
- Prefabricated fence panels
- Corrosion-resistant fence brackets
- 4d corrosion-resistant nails
- 1" corrosion-resistant deck screws
- Prefabricated gate & hardware
- Post caps
- Corrosion-resistant casing nails
- Wood sealer/ protectant or paint
- Wood blocks

1 Lay out the fence line and mark the posthole locations (inset photo). Space the holes to fit the panels you've purchased. To the length of a panel add the actual post diameter (3½" for 4" nominal posts) plus another ¼" for brackets.

2 Dig a post hole at a corner or an end post location. A clam-shell type post hole digger is a good choice for holes up to 30" deep. Make a depth gauge from scrap wood to measure the hole depth as you dig.

3 Set, plumb and brace the first post then run one of the stringers along the fence line as a reference for digging the next post hole.

4 Fill your first post hole with concrete unless you are setting posts in gravel or sand. Tamp the wet concrete with an old 2 × 4 to pack it into the post hole.

5 Attach three evenly spaced and centered fence brackets to the first post and trim fence post to desired height.

6 Set the first fence panel into the brackets, level it, and attach the end to the brackets with deck screws or joist hanger nails.

7 Position a post in the next post hole and clamp the unattached end of the fence panel to the post (you may need to tack a clamping block to the post rail first). Mark the positions of the rails onto the post. Unclamp the fence panel and remove the post from the hole.

Set the First Panel

Nail three, evenly spaced and centered fence brackets to the first post and trim fence post to desired height. The bottom of the fence needs to be at least 2" off the ground. Transfer your bracket spacing and cutoff line to a 1 × 4 gauge board with a marker. Bend down the bottom tabs on the top two brackets.

Level the panel in the brackets, supporting the loose end against the ground with blocking. Nail the brackets to the panel. For extremely gradual slopes, you may follow a mason's line that follows the actual grade instead of trying to establish true level.

Set the second post in its hole, and mark the position of the bottom bracket. Use your gauge board to mark the locations of the other brackets and post tops. Unless your fence needs to step up or down a slope, carry your measurements around the post with a speed square and mark the locations of the brackets for the next section as well.

Remove the post and attach the brackets. Trim the post top to height. Set the post in the hole and insert the stringers in the brackets. Plumb the post, make sure the panel is level and then attach the brackets to the fence panel.

Plumb the post perpendicular to the fence line with a single staked brace screwed to the post face so it will not interfere with the installation of the brackets for setting the next panel. Set the post in concrete or tamped dirt and gravel.

Top trim line

Story pole for marking bracket positions

8 Attach the fence brackets according to the marks made in the previous step. For the remaining posts, create a story pole to use as a gauge for marking consistent bracket locations and a top trim line. Trim the post to length before inserting it back into the hole.

9 Plumb the post perpendicular to the fence line, making sure the panel is level. Brace the post, recheck for plumb and level, and then set the post the same way you set the first one.

45

10 Finish installing the posts and panels. You can continue to fill the holes with concrete one at a time, or wait and fill them all once the posts are all positioned and braced.

Repeat steps 2 through 4 down the line. For a stepped fence, establish a consistent step height or determine the step-up or step-down height one panel at a time. Backfill end post and gatepost holes with concrete. Backfill the line and corner posts with concrete or tamped dirt and gravel. Allow three days for concrete to cure before removing braces.

Hang the gate (see Gates section page 130 for more information on selecting and installing gates). Attach the post caps or finials to the post tops with galvanized casing nails or deck screws. Paint, stain, or seal the fence.

11 (right) Attach post caps or finials and seal, stain or paint your new fence.

TIP: When installing a gate, attach the hinges to the gate first. For maximum strength, the hinges should be located at stringer locations on fence panels, especially if you are using strap hinges like the ones shown here. Once the hinges are attached, prop the gate into position and attach the free hinge leaves to the gate post. (A gate post should always be set in concrete—even if the other posts are loose set in gravel, sand or dirt.)

HOW TO BUILD A FACE-MOUNTED PANEL FENCE

Some types of fence panels (generally not privacy fence styles) look better and are easier to install if you attach the open stringer ends directly to the fence posts, instead of hanging them between posts.

Set and Trim the Posts

Lay out the fence line and set the posts. Space the posts the length of your panels (on-center) plus about ¼" for wiggle room. End posts, corner posts and gateposts need to be half a post diameter closer to the next post, so extends all the way across the post.

For level or nearly level fences, mark the desired post height on the end posts. Be sure to allow for at least 2" panel clearance at ground level. Stretch a mason's string between marked end posts to establish cutoff heights for line posts. Trim all posts. For stepped fences on slopes, trim the fence panel bottoms. Don't trim the post tops for a stepped panel fence until after the panels are set.

POST SPACING FOR PANEL FENCES

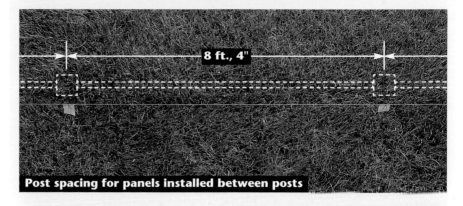

Post spacing for panels installed between posts

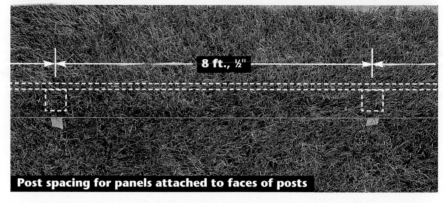

Post spacing for panels attached to faces of posts

1 Set the posts for your project. Spacing is less critical when you're attaching panels to the post faces than when you're hanging panels between posts.

2 Once the posts are installed, trim them to a consistent height, using a circular saw when possible.

3 String a mason's line across all the posts to set the height for the stringers. Check with a line level. Position one of the panels against the posts it will attach to, resting on spacer blocks that are at least 2" high.

4 Attach the first panel by driving deck screws through the ends of the stringers and into the posts. At corners and end posts, the stringers should run all the way across the post faces.

Attach the Panels

Pull a mason's line from end post to end post to establish the top line for the fence panels (the position should allow a minimum 2" clearance of panel bottoms above the ground).

Lean the first fence panel against the posts in position, with blocking underneath so it is at least 2" above the ground.

Lap stringers across the full width of end posts and half the width of line posts. Attach with two deck screws per stringer end, sized to penetrate about 2" into the post. It's always a good idea to drill pilot holes before driving the screws.

Continue down the line. If a panel joint wanders close to or past the edge of a post, add a two-foot length of bracing below each pair of butting stringers. The bracing should be the same thickness as the stringer stock.

Alternate: Attach Panels to Posts and Auxiliary Stringers

Auxiliary stringers are boards the same width and thickness as the panel stringer (often 2 × 4) that are attached to the posts to provide support for the actual panel stringers, which rest on and are attached to the auxiliary stringers.

Set and trim posts as described in Step 1, then temporarily attach your first panel with a 2" minimum ground clearance. Mark the stringer bottoms on the posts. Remove the fence panels.

Set the top edges of the auxiliary stringers to the marks. Stringers should fully overlap end posts and overlap line posts by half. Attach each stringer with a single deck screw per post, sized to penetrate the post about 2".

Make a gauge stick to mark the stringer spacing from the post top. Transfer spacing marks to all posts. Attach the remaining auxiliary stringers as described in step 2.

Rest the stringers that are pre-attached to the fence panels on top of the auxiliary stringers. Attach the fence panels to the posts with deck screws set flush with surface of the panel stringers. If a panel stringer doesn't reach all the way to a post, attach one of the panel siding boards near the post to the auxiliary stringer.

Install Gate & Attach Post Caps or Finials

Build or purchase your gate and gate hardware before you set your posts, so your gatepost spacing will be right.

Align three hinges on the gate frame so the pins are straight and they overhang the gate edge by the same amount. Attach with exterior rated screws (usually included with the gate hardware).

Shim the gate into position and screw the hinges to the post with one screw in each hinge. Test the gate, adjusting as needed to improve the swing action, and then install the remaining screws.

Attach the latch hardware according to the manufacturer instructions and test.

Attach the post caps to square-cut post tops with galvanized finish nails or deck screws, or alternately, bevel the posts tops on all four sides to create a point.

Paint, stain or seal the fence.

VARIATION: Attach auxiliary stringers directly to the posts so you can rest the panel stringers on top of them. This adds strength to the fence and also gives you some ability to compensate if the posts are a little too far apart.

5 Install the remaining panels, attach post caps or finials, and apply your finish of choice.

Post & Rail Fences

Post-and-rail construction can be used to build fences in a surprising range of styles, from a rustic split-rail fence to the more genteel post-and-rail fence.

Because they use so little lumber, post-and-rail fences are very efficient for confining a large area. In most cases you can (and probably should) build this fence by setting the posts in gravel-and-dirt footings. This method is common in some regions, but isn't appropriate everywhere. Set fence posts in concrete if required by the building codes in your area.

One other note: if you don't want to cut mortises, most lumberyards offer pre-mortised posts and tapered stringers that are designed for building split-rail fences.

Post-and rail fences, which typically are painted but sometimes stained and sealed, require more lumber and more upkeep than split rail fences, but in certain settings nothing else will do. There are endless variations on rail placement, but the directions shown on pages 52 and 53 will give you a good understanding of the basics involved. You should be able to adapt the plans and build just about any design that appeals to you.

HOW TO BUILD A POST & RAIL FENCE

Prepare the Posts

Plot the fence line and dig the postholes.

From the top of each post, measure and mark points 6" and 26½" down the center. Outline 2"-wide by 4"-tall mortises at each mark, using a cardboard template.

Cut the Mortises

Drill a series of 1" holes inside each mortise outline, drilling through the backside if necessary. Drill only halfway through for end posts, and halfway through on adjacent sides for corner posts.

Remove the remaining wood from the mortises with a hammer and chisel.

Shape the Tenons

Snap a straight chalk line down the sides of the stringers.

On one end, draw a straight line from the chalk line mark at the edge, to the center of the timber, using a combination square.

At the center, draw a 1½"-long line perpendicular to the first, extending ¾" from each side. From each end of this line, draw perpendicular lines up to the edge of the timber. You will have outlined a rough, 1½" × 1½" square tenon end.

Measure and mark 3½" down from the end stringer for the tenon length.

Rough-cut the tenons, using a reciprocating saw with a 6" wood blade. If necessary, shape the tenons with a hammer and chisel to fit the mortises.

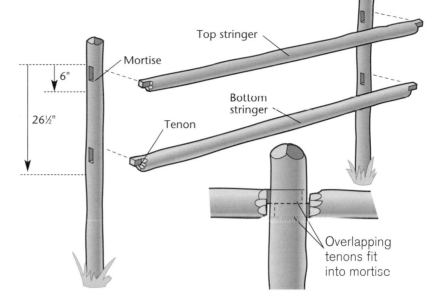

Top stringer

Mortise

26½"

6"

Tenon

Bottom stringer

Overlapping tenons fit into mortise

Set the Posts & Attach the Stringers

Fill the post holes with 6" of gravel, and insert the first post. Because each post is cut to size, make sure the post top measures 36" from the ground. If it sits too high, lay a board over the post top and tap down with a rubber mallet. If it's too low, add more gravel. Leave 6" of clearance between the position of the bottom stringer and the ground.

Begin to fill the posthole with gravel and dirt. Every few inches, tamp the dirt around the post with the end of your shovel, and check the post for plumb.

Place the next post in the post-hole without setting it. Insert the tenons of the stringers into the mortises of the first, set post. Insert the other ends of the stringers to the unset post. Adjust the post to fit the stringers if necessary.

Plumb the post and then pack the post hole with gravel, then dirt to set it. Repeat this procedure of setting a post, then attaching the stringers. Alternate the stringers so the tenons of one stringer face upward and the tenons of the next stringer face downward, creating a tight fit in the mortise. Plumb each post as you work.

1 Outline the mortise on the first fence post according to the dimensions in the illustration above. Use a cardboard template to lay out the mortise shape.

2 Remove as much waste wood as you can in the mortise area by drilling 1"-dia. holes all the way through. Square the mortises with a wood chisel.

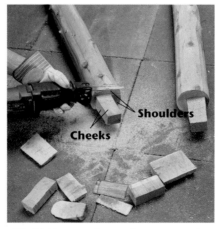

Shoulders

Cheeks

3 Using a reciprocating saw, make cheek cuts then shoulder cuts to create tenons on the ends of the rails.

4 Assemble the entire fence with the posts loose set in the post holes. Once all the rails are in place, square and plumb each section and then pack the posts in more tightly or set in concrete.

51

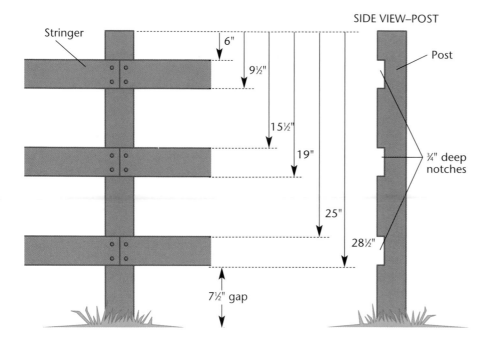

Stringer

6"

9½"

15½"

19"

25"

28½"

7½" gap

SIDE VIEW—POST

Post

¾" deep notches

SLATTED POST & RAIL FENCE

Prepare the Posts

Mark the fence line. Mark and dig postholes 72" on center.

Cut 4 × 4 posts to 66". Measure and mark at 6", 9½", 15½", 19", 25", and 28½" down from the top of two posts. Gang several posts between the marked posts and clamp them together, using bar clamps. Use a framing square to extend the marks across all the posts. Mark the notches with an "X" between pairs of marks.

Notch the Posts

Make a series of cuts inside each set of reference lines, using a circular saw with the blade cutting depth set at ¾".

Remove the remaining wood in each notch, using a hammer and chisel. Remove wood only to the depth of the original cuts so the stringers will sit flush with the face of the post.

Set the Posts & Attach Stringers

Cut the stringers to length. Paint, stain, or seal all the lumber and allow it to dry.

Brace the posts into position with the notches facing out. Run a mason's string and set a level line, keeping the notches aligned and the tops of the posts 36" above the ground. If a post is too high, lay a board over it and tap down, using a mallet or maul. If it's too low, add gravel beneath the post. Be sure there is 7½" between the bottom of the lowest notch and the ground. Set the posts in concrete and let it cure for 2 days.

Fit a stringer into the notches in the first pair of posts. Position it to cover the entire notch in the first post and half of the notch in the second. Attach the stringer, using 2" corrosion-resistant deck screws. Install the other two stringers to this pair of posts.

Butt a stringer against the first one and attach it securely. Repeat with remaining stringers.

1 Gang the posts together with the ends aligned and secure them with bar or pipe clamps. Lay out mortises for horizontal slats.

2 Make a series of ¾"-deep cuts in the waste areas using a circular saw and cutting guide. Clean out the mortises with a wood chisel.

3 Prime and paint or stain and seal the posts and rails. Assemble the fence as described in the information above.

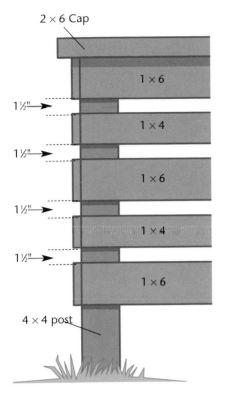

2 × 6 Cap

1 × 6

1½"

1 × 4

1½"

1 × 6

1½"

1 × 4

1½"

1 × 6

1½"

4 × 4 post

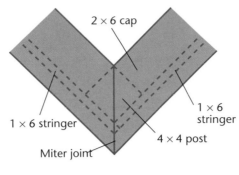

2 × 6 cap

1 × 6 stringer

1 × 6 stringer

4 × 4 post

Miter joint

TOP VIEW–DETAIL

TOOLS & MATERIALS

- Tools & materials for setting posts
- Tape measure
- Circular saw
- Combination square
- Drill
- Lumber
- 2" and 3" deck screws
- Paint, stain, or sealer

HOW TO BUILD A CAPPED POST & RAIL FENCE

Set the Posts

Mark the fence line, spacing posts 72" on center. Cut the lumber to size. Paint, stain, or seal the posts and let them dry. Dig post holes and set the posts. Let concrete cure for 2 days.

Measure and mark each post 36" above the ground. Trim to height with a circular saw or handsaw. Touch up the finish on top of the posts.

Mark a line down the center of the outside face of each post (except the end or gate posts).

Attach the Stringers

Measure from the reference line on one post to the line on the next. For each bay, cut two 1 × 4s and three 1 × 6s to this length. For the last bay, measure from the last reference line to the outside edge of the end post. Paint, stain, or seal the stringers.

Position a 1 × 6 against the faces of two posts with its top edge flush with the top of the posts and its ends flush with the reference lines. Clamp the stringer in place, then

attach it on both ends, using pairs of 2" deck screws.

On each post, mark a line 1½" from the bottom of the 1 × 6. Position and attach a 1 × 4 as described above. Alternate 1 × 6s and 1 × 4s, spacing them 1½" apart.

Attach the Cap Stringer

Measure and cut 2 × 6s to fit between post tops. Add 1¾" on the end posts so the cap stringers extend beyond the posts. For corners, miter-cut the ends at 45° angles, using a circular saw.

Position a cap stringer on the post tops, flush with the back of the posts and extending 1¼" beyond the front. Make sure the ends are centered on the posts. Attach caps with 3" deck screws.

1 Set posts and mark a vertical centerline on post faces where rails will butt together (use a combination square as a pencil guide).

2 Install horizontal rails, butting ends together and maintaining an even gap between rails.

3 Cut cap boards to length and attach to the tops of the fence posts, mitering the caps at corners.

Virginia Rail Fences

The Virginia Rail Fence—also called a worm, snake, and zigzag fence—was actually considered the national fence by the U.S. Department of Agriculture prior to the advent of wire fences in the late 1800s. All states with farmland cleared from forests had them in abundance.

The simplest fences were built with an extreme zig-zag, and didn't require posts. To save on lumber and land, farmers began straightening the fences and burying pairs of posts at the rail junctures. A variation in design that emerged with entirely straight lines is called a Kentucky Rail fence.

Feel free to accommodate the overlapping rail fence we build here to suit your tastes and needs. Increase the zig-zag to climb rolling ground, decrease it to stretch the fence out. Lapped rail fences should be made from rot resistant wood, like cedar, locust, or cyprus.

For the most authentic looking fence, try to find split, rather than sawn logs. For longevity, raise the bottom rail off the ground with stones. Posts may eventually rot below ground, but the inherently stable zig-zag form should keep the fence standing until you can replace them.

HOW TO BUILD A VIRGINIA RAIL FENCE

Play With Your Rails

Lay out three or four sections of fence rails without posts along your fence line to get a sense of how much overlap, zig-zag, and height you want.

Vary the side-to-side offset of the rail junctures. More extreme zig-zags accommodate rolling land better and are more stable, but they require more space and lumber.

Vary the height of your prototype. Be aware that your finished fence will ride higher, when the rails are set on top of rocks or wired between posts and shimmed.

Mark Your Postholes

Lay out the outside border of your fence. This is the line that you don't want any part of your fence to cross.

Run two parallel mason's strings 6" and 24" inside your outside border, from end to end of the

The Virginia Rail Fence exhibits a very familar style to anyone who has spent much time in countryside that was cleared and farmed in the 18th and 19th Centuries. Since nails were scarce, these zig-zagging post-and-rail fences were popular because they are held together with only wire or rope.

1 Lay out a straight line to roughly mark the desired fenceline. Then use marking paint to draw reference lines 2 ft. away from the fenceline in each side. These indicate the outside borders of the fence structure.

fenceline. Subtract two feet from your rail length. This is the approximate distance each fence section will cover along your fence line, providing for rail overlap and a slight zig-zag. Adjust this section length so it divides into the length of your fence line.

Starting at one end of your outer line, mark off 16 ft. increments on the ground with nails through plastic flagging. Starting at the same end of the your inner line, make the first mark at 8 ft. and then mark 16 ft. increments to the end.

Check with a marked stick to see that your zig-zag post spacing is a little over 8 ft. apart. Rail overlap can be as little as 8" per rail end.

Set Posts and First Rail

Dig postholes three times the width of one post to 18" to 24" deep, using a posthole digger (manual or power). It's not necessary for the postholes to reach the frost line.

Place two posts in each hole. There should be room for a rail to pass between the posts in the fence line. Plumb the posts and pack dirt into the holes.

Thread bottom rails into posts in alternate bays so the fence will stay level. Use large, twisted, less-regular rails for the bottoms. Prop the rails up off the ground on rocks. Cinch the post tops together with rope to keep them parallel.

2 Run additional mason's lines parallel to the fenceline and 12" away from it on each side. Calculate the optimal length of each bay and make marks along the mason's lines at each increment (the increment is 8 ft. in the project shown above).

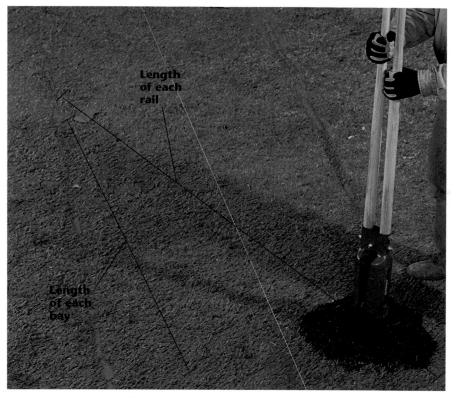

Length of each rail

Length of each bay

3 Postholes should be 18" to 24" deep and about three times the diameter of the posts in width.

Set Remaining Rails and Bind

Lay the remaining rails alternately. You can use chunks of wood split from the post-top trimmings as spacers to level the rails. Save heavier rails for the tops.

Cinch the post tops tight together with your rope. Wrap 9-gauge galvanized wire a couple of times around the posts below the rope, directly on top of the top rails. Leave longish tails for leverage. Twist the tails a couple of full turns. Stick a large screwdriver under the twist, and rotate it close to a full turn or until the wire bites into the wood and your rope goes slack. Remove ropes, trim the wires and pound wire ends into the posts for safety.

Trim off posts square. Use a heavy, long-handled maul to pound the posts in about 6" or until the fence is stiff. Stand on something stable to bring the post tops to waist height while pounding. Paint with wood sealer or leave it to age.

4 Loosely position a pair of posts in each holes, using backfill dirt to separate them an amount that's roughly equal to the rail thickness.

5 Position a rock near each post set to support the bottom rails and then insert the rail between the posts pairs so it extends past the posts an equal amount at each end.

6 Install the remaining rails between post pairs, staggering them as you go. The post tops should be cinched with rope to keep them from spreading.

7 Once the fence rails and posts are all installed, bind the tops and bottoms of each post pair with 9-gauge galvanized wire.

8 Insert the blade of a heavy-duty screwdriver between the binding wires and twist it to tighten the wires (as if you're applying a tourniquet).

9 If the post-and-rail structure feels loose at any of the lapped unions, try driving the posts a bit deeper into the ground. Protect the post tops with a wood block.

Composite fencing is manufactured with a blend of wood fibers and plastic resins. It is denser than PVC-only fencing and available in a wider range of colors and textures, with some doing a fairly convincing job of replicating the look of real wood. The privacy fence above is from the Seclusions line by Trex.

Vinyl & Composite Fences

Vinyl and composite fences require little mainte-nance and can last a lifetime (if they don't get hit by a truck or caught in a brushfire). This low-maintenance longevity justifies the high initial cost for many. Manufacturers of both vinyl and composite fences claim that they are less expensive than wood in the long run, when you factor in the repair, refinishing, and even-tual replacement of wood fences as the years pass.

Vinyl fences are made from polyvinyl chloride (PVC), the same plastic used in vinyl house siding and waste pipes. Vinyl fencing is co-extruded with an outside layer that includes titanium dioxide. This is the same compound found in sunscreen, and protects the plastic from degrada-tion by ultra-violet (U.V.) sunrays. Because titanium diox-ide is white, vinyl fencing is most commonly available in

bright white, although PVC products with light tan and gray coloring are starting to hit the market.

Composite fences are made from a blend of wood fibers and plastic resins (some resins are recycled from grocery bags). The wood fiber provides strength and U.V. protec-tion while the plastic keeps the material from absorbing water and rotting. In the world of synthetic fences, com-posite fence manufacturers claim the environmental high ground. The manufacturing of composite lumber has not been linked to dioxin pollution, as PVC production has been. Composites can also be produced in darker colors than PVC and with an assortment of surface textures.

Vinyl fencing has been around longer than composite fencing, and comes in almost as many styles as wood fenc-ing. Traditionally, after constructing a vinyl fence, rebar

"Traditional" vinyl fences are gleaming white when installed, but the color mellows a bit after a year or two of exposure to the elements.

rods were put into some or all of the hollow posts and the posts were filled partway with concrete. This is still the way most pros build vinyl fences. DIY-friendly vinyl and composite fences are available with posts that are essentially hollow sleeves designed to fit over standard pressure-treated 4 × 4 posts.

Vinyl and composite fencing is assembled from pre-manufactured components and panels. This makes it difficult to adjust the length of fence sections, should your post spacing be off. (You can cut the rails, but you can't increase their length). For this reason, you need to either set the posts as you go or be very meticulous with your all-at-the-same-time post spacing and leveling. If the terrain is uneven or the soil is full of roots or rocks, consider setting one post at a time.

Unless you have a fondness for that well-lived look, consider doing away with major fence maintenance forever by replacing your painted wood pickets with a vinyl or composite fence system.

Vinyl fences have exploded in popularity in recent years because they require virtually no maintenance other than an occasional hosing down.

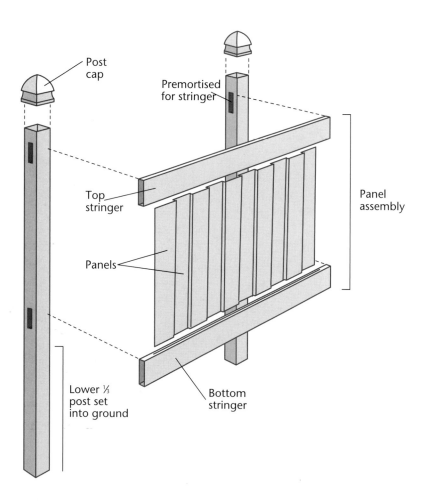

Post cap

Post cap

Premortised for stringer

Top stringer

Panels

Panel assembly

Bottom stringer

Lower ⅓ post set into ground

HOW TO INSTALL VINYL FENCING

Note: These are general installation tips. Refer to the manufacturer's instructions for your specific fence style.

Prepare the Materials

Mark the fence line on your property, using stakes to indicate corner and end post locations. Roughly locate gates.

Map out your fence on paper. Measure and record distances between corner posts and end posts. On sloped land, measure your distances along a level line rather than along the grade.

Bring your map to a fence supplier. They will work up a materials list. Order your fence.

Order dry concrete mix and other supplies according to fence supplier formulas. Keep concrete well covered and protected from ground moisture. Rent a drum mixer for the day of construction.

Establish Post Locations

Establish center-to-center gatepost spacing by adding the width of the gate, the space required by hinge and latch hardware and the actual diameter of one post.

Determine center-to-center line post spacing by adding the length of a panel to the width of a post. Normally, you'll need to add around ¼" for the brackets.

Establish exact post locations using a mason's string and batter boards. Before removing the mason's line, record its position on your batter boards and, when marking an end post, also note the distance from the post end to the batter board.

Dig First Post Holes

Dig the first four holes in a run at least to the minimum depth required by your fence height plus 6" for drainage gravel. If drilling the holes with an auger, use a 10"-dia. blade for a 4" post and a 12" blade for a 5" post.

Tamp about 6" of pea gravel in the bottom of each hole, bringing it up to the level needed to provide desired bottom rail clearance. For frost footings, the post doesn't need to reach the gravel.

Position the post-face strings between pairs of batter boards and mark the location of line posts on the string. Dig postholes.

Assemble the panels

Place tape over the ends of the lower stringers so concrete cannot seep into them from the posts. Insert the panel pieces into the prerouted holes of the bottom stringer. Make sure each piece fits securely. If not, add duct tape to the bottom of the pieces so the fit is tighter. Attach the top stringer to the panels, making sure the fit is tight. Work from one end and adjust the panel pieces to fit into the prerouted holes. Secure the stringer to the panels with the self-tapping screws provided by the manufacturer.

Set the First Post

Position the first post. Because the posts are manufactured to size, the posts must sit precisely at the height of the fence. If a post is too high, lay a board over the top and gently tap it down. If it's too low, add gravel beneath it. Leave enough room for a 2" gap between the bottom of the fence and the ground. Mix

concrete and set the post. Use a level on adjacent sides to check that the post is plumb. Keep the posts plumb with 2 × 4 braces attached to stakes driven into the ground. Duct tape is strong enough to hold the braces to the vinyl posts without causing any damage. Let the concrete cure at least two days.

Attach the Panels

Set the next post and pour the concrete footing but do not brace the post just yet. With the assistance of another person, fit the panel between the posts. Insert the top and bottom stringers to the prerouted holes of

TOOLS & MATERIALS
- Tools & materials for setting posts
- Cordless drill or screwdriver
- Level
- Vinyl fencing materials
- Duct tape
- #3 rebar
- Rebar separator clips
- Construction adhesive
- Hacksaw

1 Cover the ends of the lower stringers with duct tape so the concrete cannot seep into them when it is poured into the posts.

2 Attach the individual strips by working from one end and adjusting them to fit into the pre-routed holes of the bottom stringer.

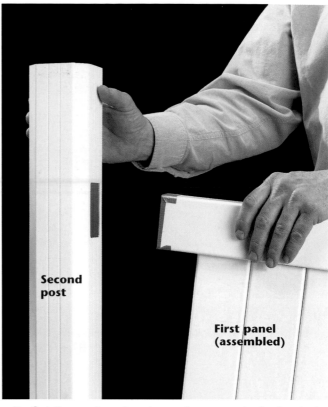

3 Set the first fence post. Keep the posts plumb with 2 × 4 braces attached to stakes driven into the ground. Duct tape is strong enough to hold the braces to the vinyl posts without causing any damage. Fill with concrete.

4 Set the next post and pour the concrete footing but do not brace the post just yet. With the assistance of another person, fit the assembled panel between the posts, and then plumb, level and brace the second post.

Shown cut away for clarity

5 Install the second assembled panel. Attach panels with screws driven through brackets as you go.

6 Fill posts with concrete as they are readied. Concrete for line posts need only come up to roughly ground level.

Shown cut away for clarity

TIP: While wood-reinforced vinyl fencing is gaining ground with do-it-yourselfers, much vinyl fencing is still reinforced with concrete. With this style, rails or stringers are pushed into holes in the hollow posts, rebar (textured steel rod) is inserted in posts needing extra support and concrete is poured in the post tops. The concrete envelops the rebar, the rail ends, and any fasteners driven into the post, such as those holding the hinges.

the first (previously set) post. Insert the stringers on the other end of the panel into the next post. If necessary, adjust the post to accommodate the stringers.

Inside the post, drive a screw (provided with the kit) through the top stringer to secure it. Plumb the post and brace it with 2 × 4s. Repeat this procedure of setting a post, then attaching a panel. Plumb each post and brace it securely in place before you begin work on the next panel.

Reinforce the End Posts & Corner Posts

If you're installing a gate, mount the hinge and latch hardware to the gate posts. Attach the gate.

Connect two 72"-lengths of #3 (⅜" dia.) rebar with rebar-separator clips for every end and corner post. Place one clip 6" down from the top of each piece and another 12" up from the bottom. Position the rebar assembly inside the post, with the pieces of rebar sitting in opposing corners. Fill the post with concrete, leaving at least 6" of exposed rebar at the top. Wipe off any excess concrete.

Attach the Post Caps

Attach post caps with glue or screws, if provided by the manufacturer. If you use glue, apply it to the inside edge of the cap, and then attach the cap to the post top. Wipe off any excess glue as soon as possible. Cover exposed screw heads with screw caps if provided. Wash the fence with a mild detergent and water.

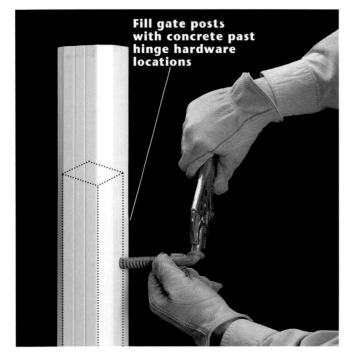

Fill gate posts with concrete past hinge hardware locations

7 If you're installing a gate, drive any gate hanging hardware or fasteners into the gatepost before filling the hollow post sleeve with concrete.

8 Attach post caps with glue.

New composite fencing systems offer a broader range of colors and employ installation techniques that are more familiar to DIYers than most vinyl fencing.

The composite fence system shown here is anchored by hollow post sleeves that are fitted over 4 × 4 posts set in concrete. Bottom stringers are fashioned from aluminum rails clad with composite material. Siding infill fits into a channel in the bottom stringer and the end strip is screwed to the post. A top stringer fits over the tops of the siding and is supported by brackets attached to the posts. Post caps cover the post sleeves.

HOW TO INSTALL A COMPOSITE FENCE

The following instructions offer general information on installing a fence system with hollow posts that fit over 4 × 4 posts. The specific model shown is "Seclusions" manufactured by Trex. Refer to the manufacturer's instructions for whichever fence type you purchase.

Obtain Materials, Locate Posts

Obtain your materials and mark your exact post locations as you would for a vinyl fence. This particular fence required 96" on-center spacing of line posts.

Read "Handling Slope" if your fenceline slopes. Post spacing is measured along the grade for level and contoured fences and along a level line for stepped fences.

Position gateposts correctly. For this fence, on-center gatepost spacing equals the width of the gate, plus 1" plus the post width.

Dig Postholes, Set Posts

Slip composite post sleeves over 4 × 4 pressure treated posts. The posts do not need to reach to the full height of the sleeves, but they should extend into the concrete footing and well up into the sleeve. Set your posts in 30" holes on 6" of pea gravel. Be meticulous with post spacing, alignment and plumbing: the rails are difficult to cut down and cannot be lengthened.

Set posts to the manufacturer-specified height as well. Fences stepped down a hill need to be set higher above the grade.

Tamp wet concrete mix into your post holes with a 2 × 4, to within 2" or 3" inches of the top of the hole. Let cure for two to three days before removing your bracing.

Install the Brackets

Screw the bottom bracket to the post with the fasteners provided. The manufacturer of the system shown here provides a template for attaching the brackets that sets the bottom stringer 2" up from the ground.

Measure up from the bottom bracket to establish the position of the top bracket according to manufacturer specifications.

For a level fence or a fence that follows the contour of the land, all bottom brackets are set the same height above grade.

For a stepped fence, attach the brackets for a fence section to the up-slope post first. Draw a level line from the bottom of the lower bracket to position the lower bracket on the downhill post.

Install Bottom Rails

Slide the two bottom rail sides over the aluminum bottom rail insert. For short sections, the composite part of the rail may be cut down with a carbide tooth circular saw blade. Cut the aluminum insert with a non-ferrous metal cutting blade in your circular saw.

Place the bottom rail onto the lower brackets. Attach each side of the rail insert to its bracket with a screw provided for the purpose.

Install Pickets

Notch first picket in each 8 ft. section in order to avoid upper bracket assembly. Secure the picket to the post with three of the picket screws, evenly spaced.

Insert each C-shaped picket into the bottom rail so it opposes and interconnects with the last. Continue until you reach the far post. A full section of our fence used 19 pickets, and would require less if it's been cut down.

Notch the upper corner of the last picket to clear the bracket. Secure the last picket to the post the same way you attached the first picket, with three evenly spaced screws into the post.

Install Top Rail, Post Caps, and Gate

Place the top rail over the pickets and upper brackets. Screw the rail to each bracket with a rail-to-bracket screw.

Install the post caps with 8d galvanized casing nails or glue it on with exterior-rated adhesive.

Install gate according to manufacturer instructions.

1 Lay out the fenceline with batterboards and strings and then begin digging postholes at the post locations. Start at an end or corner.

2 Insert 4 × 4 pressure-treated wood posts into composite post sleeves and set the posts in concrete. Plumb, level and brace the posts as with vinyl posts.

TOOLS & MATERIALS

- Tools & materials for setting posts
- Cordless drill or screwdriver
- Level
- Composite fencing materials
- Duct tape
- #3 rebar
- Rebar separator clips
- Construction adhesive

3 Set all posts and check post heights with a mason's line or laser level. Trim to uniform height if needed. Attach hanger brackets according to manufacturer's directions—some will supply alignment templates (inset photo).

4 Assemble the bottom stringer. Since composite material is not structurally rated, systems use either metal or wood reinforcement. Assemble the stringers (here, composite cladding is threaded over both faces of an aluminum rail).

5 If stringers are too long or if you need to reduce the size of section to fit a small bay, cut the rail with a saw appropriate to the material (a hacksaw or a circular saw with a nonferrous metal blade may be used to cut aluminum). The composite components may be cut with a circular saw or power miter saw and a panel-cutting blade.

6 Rest the clad rail stringers onto the post brackets and check with a level. If necessary, remove the stringer and adjust the bracket height.

7 Attach each side of the rail insert to its bracket with a screw provided for the purpose.

8 The initial siding strip fits inside the upper bracket and is screwed to the fence post.

9 Begin installing the interlocking (inset photo) siding strips. Trim off the corner of the first infill picket in each section in order to avoid upper bracket assembly. Set the siding into the lower stringer channel and secure the first strip to its post with screws provided by the manufacturer.

10 Continue filling in with the interlocking siding strips.

11 Trim the upper corner of the last picket to clear the bracket. Secure last picket to the post like the first, with three evenly spaced screws into the post.

12 Place the top rail over the pickets and upper brackets.

13 From above, screw the top rail to each bracket with a rail-to-bracket screw.

14 Install the post caps with 2" galvanized casing nails, or with a multi-purpose wood glue, such as Gorilla Glue or Liquid Nails. Faceted pyramid caps and flat-topped caps are available.

Ornamental Metal

Today's ornamental metal fences are designed to replicate the elegant wrought-iron designs of the past. They are made of aluminum and galvanized steel, with a powder-coat finish to help prevent rust. Styles range from the simple to the ornate, and are available in a variety of colors and sizes. These fences have become recent favorites for swimming pool enclosures.

Few home centers stock these materials, but some may be able to order them for you. Many manufacturers and distributors maintain web sites where you can get more information or place orders. A quick search of the internet should yield plenty of options.

As with any prefabricated fence, always read the manufacturer's instructions thoroughly before beginning installation. Installing these fences is generally simple, but does require two people.

The fence sections are manufactured or welded together in 48"- to 96"-long sections, and the posts are pre-cut. In our design, the posts have pre-routed holes for the stringer ends. Other designs use systems of brackets or fasteners.

If a fence section is too long, cut it to fit, using a hacksaw. Make sure to cut off only as much as necessary—it's vital to maintain a tight fit and proper spacing.

When slope is an issue, metal fencing can be contoured with the ground if the grade's rise is less then 12" over a 72" run. Anything greater will require stepping the fence. If you're using brackets, simply determine the step measurement and set the brackets accordingly. Any routed holes in the posts will have to be cut on site.

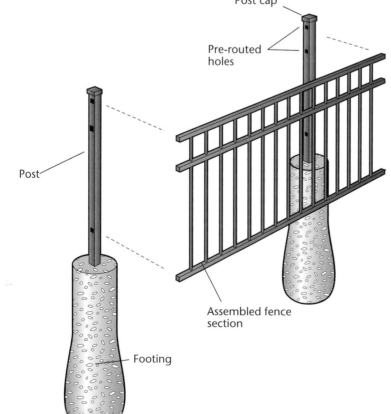

Post cap

Pre-routed holes

Post

Assembled fence section

Footing

HOW TO INSTALL AN ORNAMENTAL METAL FENCE

NOTE: These are general installation tips. Refer to the manufacturer's instructions for your specific fence.

Set the First Post

Lay out and check the materials to be sure you have all the parts and hardware.

Mark the fence line with stakes and mason's string . Space and dig the postholes according to local codes and the manufacturer's recommendations.

Starting with a gate or end post, set the first post in place. Use a level to make sure the post is plumb on adjacent sides. Brace it with stakes and scrap pieces of 2 × 4 tied or taped to the post.

Because the posts are manufactured to size, the top of the post must be at fence height when it's set. Measure the height; if the post is too high, lay a board over it and gently tap it down, using a rubber mallet. If it's too low, add gravel beneath it.

Set the post in concrete. Let the concrete cure—you'll use this post as a starting point for the remaining sections of the fence.

Attach the Panels

Set the next post in concrete, but don't brace it yet.

With the assistance of another person, insert the top and bottom stringers of a fence section to the pre-routed holes of the fixed end or gate post.

At the other end of the section, insert the stringer ends to the line post. If necessary, adjust the line post to accommodate the stringers.

For the corners, attach the first section, then trim the stringer ends of the adjacent section approximately 1", using a hacksaw, so the sections remain properly spaced.

Finish the Installation

Drive 1" self-tapping screws through the posts and into each stringer end to secure the fence sections to the posts.

Plumb the line post and brace it firmly, using 2 × 4s on adjacent sides.

Continue setting posts and attaching sections of fence, plumbing each post as you go. Let the concrete cure for at least 24 hours.

Attach finials to the posts, using a rubber mallet or set screws, if provided.

1 Dig post holes and set the first post in concrete. Brace it with 2 × 4s on adjacent sides.

2 Insert the stringer ends of the fence section into the routed holes of the posts.

3 Secure the stringers to the posts with 1" self-tapping screws.

Chain Link Fencing

If you're looking for a strong, durable, and economical way to keep pets and children in—or out—of your yard, a chain link fence may be the perfect solution. Chain link fences require minimal maintenance and provide excellent security. Erecting a chain link fence is relatively easy, especially on level property. Leave contoured fence lines to the pros. For a chain link fence with real architectural beauty, consider a California style chain link with wood posts and rails. We show you how on page 136. To change the look and function of a chain link fence, consider the treatments reviewed on pages 77 and 81.

A 48"-tall fence—the most common choice for residential use—is what we've demonstrated here. The posts, fittings, and chain link mesh, which are made from galvanized metal, can be purchased at home centers and fencing retailers. The end, corner, and gate posts, called terminal posts, bear the stress of the entire fence line. They're larger in diameter than line posts and require larger concrete footings. A footing three times the post diameter is sufficient for terminal posts. A properly installed stringer takes considerable stress off the end posts by holding the post tops apart.

The fittings are designed to accommodate slight alignment and height differences between terminal posts and line posts. Tension bands, which hold the mesh to the terminal posts, have one flat side to keep the mesh flush along the outside of the fence line. The stringer ends hold the top stringer in place and keep it aligned. Loop caps on the line posts position the top stringer to brace the mesh.

When the framework is in place, the mesh must be tightened against it. This is done a section at a time with a winch tool called a come-along. As you tighten the come-along, the tension is distributed evenly across the entire length of the mesh, stretching it taut against the framework. One note of caution: It's surprisingly easy to topple the posts if you over-tighten the come-along. To avoid this problem, tighten just until the links of the mesh are difficult to to squeeze together by hand.

To stiffen the fabric along the bottom, you may add a tension wire close to the ground before installing the fabric. This is more important on vinyl coated chain link, which is more flexible.

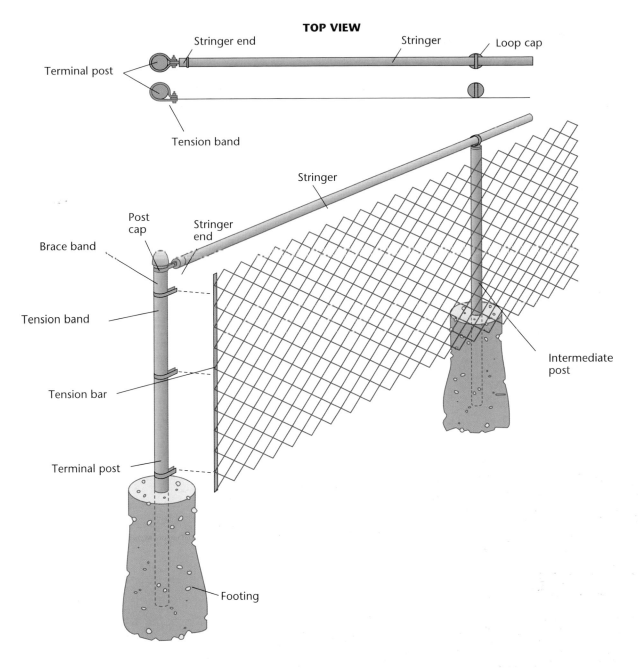

TOP VIEW

Terminal post

Stringer end

Stringer

Loop cap

Tension band

Stringer

Post cap

Brace band

Stringer end

Tension band

Tension bar

Terminal post

Intermediate post

Footing

HOW TO INSTALL A CHAIN LINK FENCE

Set the Posts

Mark the fence location with stakes and mason's string. Measure and mark the post locations every 96" on center.

Dig postholes 30 inches down or below the frost line, whichever is deeper. Line posts should be 6 inches wide but terminal (end, corner and gate) posts should be 8-inches wide and belled even wider at the bottoms. You may adjust line postholes along (but not out of) the fence line to avoid obstacles.

Set the terminal posts in concrete, but leave the top of the concrete about three inches down from grade level. Each terminal post should be 50" above the ground or two inches above the fence height. Plumb each post and

TOOLS & MATERIALS

- Tools & materials for setting posts
- Tape measure
- Mason's string
- Stakes
- Chalk
- Wrench & pliers
- Hacksaw or pipe cutter
- Come-along (fence stretcher)
- Duct tape
- Galvanized terminal and line posts
- Galvanized fittings (see diagram)
- Bolts & nuts for chain link fence assembly
- Galvanized chain link mesh

brace it on adjacent sides with staked braces taped securely to post. Make sure gate posts are spaced for your gate and gate hardware. Pack dirt over concrete.

Mark each terminal post 46" above grade. Run a mason's string at this level as a line-post height reference. Run another mason's string along the outside face of the terminal posts near the ground. Adjust line post-holes now if needed.

Set line posts along (but not touching) bottom mason's line. Keep the post tops about 46-in. above grade, but if they diverge from your height line, make sure they do so gradually and evenly. Divergence will bring the fabric into the ground or cause gaps at the bottom. Plum each post and brace it on adjacent sides.

Site down the posts to check for dips and bumps. Fill the line postholes with concrete to about three inches below grade. Pack dirt over the concrete and allow to cure for a day or two..

Attach the Fittings

Add a fourth tension band at the bottom, oriented like the others, if you will be using a tension wire.

For corner posts, use six tension bands—two bands in each location with flat sides to the outside of the fence and pointing away from each other. Add two more opposing bands to the bottom for a tension wire.

Attach the Top Stringer

Start at one section, between two terminal posts, and feed the non-tapered end of a top stringer piece through the loop caps, toward a terminal post. Insert the non-tapered end into the cup of the stringer end. Make sure the stringer is snug. If necessary, loosen the brace band bolt and adjust it.

Continue to feed pieces of top stringer through the loop caps, fitting the non-tapered ends over the tapered ends. Use a sleeve to join two non-tapered ends, if necessary.

To fit the last piece of top stringer in the section, measure from where the taper begins on the previous piece to the inside back wall of the stringer end cup. Cut a piece of top stringer to size, using a hacksaw or pipe cutter. Connect the non-tapered end to the tapered end of the previous stringer. Loosen the brace band bolt and insert the cut end to the stringer end assembly. Make sure the fittings remain snug. Repeat for each section of the fence.

HOW TO INSTALL A CHAIN LINK FENCE

1 Set the posts and brace them into position so they are plumb. Chain link fence posts should be set in concrete.

2 Place three tension bands on every gate and end post. Place the first band 8" from the top, the second 24" from the top, and the third 8" off the ground. Make sure the flat side of each tension band faces the outside of the fence and points into the fence bay.

74

3 For a corner, place two brace bands 3" from the top of the post. Attach stringer ends with the angle side up to the upper brace band, and the angle side down to the lower band.

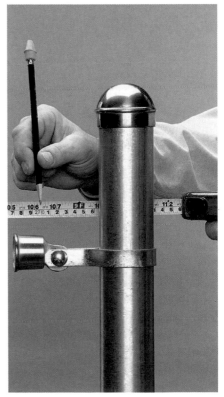

4 Top each terminal post with a post cap and each line post with a loop cap. Make sure the loop cap openings are perpendicular to the fence line, with the offset side facing the outside of the fence line.

5 Cut the last piece of top stringer in a section to size. Adjust the brace band and stringer end to fit it in place.

6 To fit the last piece of top stringer in the section, measure from where the taper begins on the previous piece to the inside back wall of the stringer end cup. Cut a piece of top stringer to fit.

Apply Tension Wire and Fabric

Add a tension wire to the fence between lower tension bands according to manufacturer instructions. You will need a wire grip for your come-along.

Weave a tension bar through the end row of the mesh. Secure the tension bar to the tension bands on the terminal post with bolts and nuts. Make sure the bolt heads face the outside of the fence.

Pull the mesh taut along the fence line by hand, moving towards the terminal post at the other end. Set the mesh on end and lean it against the posts as you go.

Stretch the Chain Link Mesh

Weave the spread bar for a come-along through the mesh, approximately 48" from the final terminal post. Hook the spread bar of the come-along to the tension bar. Attach the other end of the come-along to the terminal post, roughly in the middle.

Tighten the come-along until you can't squeeze the diamonds together with one hand. Make sure to keep the top of the mesh lined up, so that the peaks of the links rise about 1" above the top stringer.

Pull the remaining chain link mesh tight to the terminal post by hand, and insert a tension bar where the mesh meets the tension braces.

Remove any excess mesh by bending back both knuckle ends of one zig-zag strand in the mesh. Spin the strand counter-clockwise so it winds out of the links, separating the mesh into two.

Secure the tension bar to the tension bands with bolts and nuts, with the bolt heads facing the outside of the fence.

Use tie wire spaced every 12" to attach the mesh to the top stringer and line posts. Use hog rings and hog ring pliers to attach the fabric to the tension wires. Repeat for each section.

7 Weave a tension bar through the chain link mesh and attach it to the tension braces with bolts.

8 Use a come-along to stretch the mesh taut against the fence. The mesh is tight enough when the links are difficult to squeeze together by hand.

TIP: WEAVING CHAIN LINK MESH TOGETHER

If a section of chain link mesh comes up short between the terminal posts, you can add another piece by weaving two sections together.

With the first section laid out along the fence line, estimate how much more mesh is needed to reach the next terminal post. Over-estimate 6" or so, so you don't come up short again.

Detach the amount of mesh needed from the new roll by bending back the knuckle ends of one zig-zag strand in the mesh. Make sure the knuckles of the same strand are undone at the top and bottom of the fence. Spin the strand counter-clockwise to wind it out of the links, separating the mesh into two.

Place this new section of chain link at the short end of the mesh so the zig-zag patterns of the links line up with one another.

Weave the new section of chain link into the other section by reversing the unwinding process. Hook the end of the strand into the first link of the first section. Spin the strand clockwise until it winds into the first link of the second section, and so on. When the strand has connected the two sections, bend both ends back into a knuckle. Now you can attach the chain link mesh to the fence framework.

TIP: HANG WOOD FENCE PANELS ON CHAIN LINK POSTS

Chain link fences are inexpensive and can be erected quickly once you've got the hang of it, but they do not necessarily conform to everyone's idea of good-looking. If you're looking for a quick and easy way to replace your chain link fence without having to remove and replace all the posts, why not re-use the chain link posts in a wood fence?

Major wood hanger hardware manufacturers offer special hardware that is designed to let you attach a prefabricated wood panel directly to a chain link fence post. You could also use the hanger hardware to attach bare stringer so you can fill in with any siding you prefer, even including some types of vinyl or composite siding.

For more information on fence hanger hardware, see the Resources section.

HOW TO BUILD A CALIFORNIA-STYLE CHAIN LINK FENCE

Build the Frame

Lay out your fence line and set 4 × 4 posts at a regular spacing between six and eight feet on center (ref. setting posts).

Trim posts (ref. trimming sequence in How to Contour a Fence) to 4 inches higher than your chain link fabric.

Clamp, mark, cut and toenail 2 × 4 top stringers with the top edge 4" down from post tops. Use 16d galvanized nails. Pre-drill nail holes in stringers if necessary.

Attach optional bottom stringers 2" up from the ground for a more secure fence at the base.

Add Tension Wire, Accessories

Instead of a bottom rail, draw a tension wire about an inch up from the fence bottom between end posts on the fabric side. You may gently tighten with a come along according to fencing manufacturers directives.

Wrap tension wire around end posts. Double wire back over and anchoring staple and staple again. Staple wire at line posts.

Attach post caps.

Seal, or stain and seal, the fence framing.

Note: pressure treated lumber that's not kiln dried after treatment (KDAT) may need to air dry for a year before it will accept finishes.

Attach the Chain Link

Run a Tension bar through the last weave of fencing and nail to the end post with large H.D. galvanized staples every eight inches.

If the fence is on a slope, temporarily hang part of the fabric from the rail and mark off the weaves (zig zag strands of wire) that need to be trimmed and unwound from the fabric so that the tension bar may be threaded through the diamonds parallel to the post.

Unroll the fabric down toward the last post and adjust the weaves so they are even. Stretch the fabric gently with the come-along.

Thread a tension bar at the last post and attach it with staples every eight inches.

Staple the fabric to the line posts every foot and rails every two feet. Attach fabric to tension wire every two feet with hog rings using hog ring pliers

1 Lay out your fence line and set 4 × 4 posts at a regular spacing between six and eight feet on center (see page 22).

2 Trim posts to 4 inches higher than your chain link fabric.

3 Clamp, mark, cut and toenail 2 × 4 top stringers with the top edge 4" down from post tops. Use 16d H.D. galvanized nails. Pre-drill nail holes in stringers if necessary.

4 Instead of a bottom rail, draw a tension wire about an inch up from the fence bottom between end posts on the fabric side. You may gently tighten with a come-along according to fencing manufacturers directives.

5 Wrap tension wire around end posts. Double wire back over and anchoring staple and staple again. Staple wire at line posts.

6 Attach a post cap or finial made from the same species wood as the posts and stringers.

7 Run a tension bar through the last weave of fencing and nail to the end post with large H.D. galvanized staples every eight inches.

8 Unroll the fabric down toward the last post and adjust the weaves so they are even. Stretch the fabric gently with the come-along.

9 Thread a tension bar at the last post and attach it with staples every eight inches.

Privacy fabric tape cuts the wind and provides partial privacy. It's purchased in rolls with a limited number of color options. It is relatively inexpensive, but threading it through the chain link fabric is time consuming.

Vinyl privacy slats create vertical lines and are easier to install than tape. They're available in a limited number of colors at most building centers. Some varieties of strips also have a grass-like texture.

Brick & Cedar

This elegant fence is not nearly as difficult to construct as it looks. It does, however, require some time and effort, and will make use of both your carpentry and masonry skills. There are also quite a few necessary materials, which does increase the expense. But when the project is complete, you'll have an attractive, durable structure that will be the envy of the neighborhood.

The 72" brick pillars replace the posts of most fences. The footings need to be 4" longer and wider than the pillar on each side, 16 × 20" for this project.

To maintain an even ⅜" mortar joint spacing between bricks, create a story pole using a 2 × 2 marked with the spacing. After every few courses, hold the pole against the pillar to check the joints for a consistent thickness. Also make sure the pillars remain as plumb, level, and square as possible. Poor pillar construction greatly reduces strength and longevity of the pillars.

Attaching the stringers to the pillars is much easier than you may imagine. Fence brackets and concrete screws are available that have as much holding power as lag bolts and anchors. Although other brands are available, we used ¼"-dia. TapCon concrete screws. The screws come with a special drill bit to make sure the embedment holes are the right diameter and depth, which simplifies the process for you.

The part of this project that looks the trickiest is creating the arched top of the cedar-slat fence sections. It can be achieved relatively easily by using a piece of PVC pipe. With the ends anchored, the pipe is flexible enough to bend into position and rigid enough to hold the form of the arch so it can be traced.

HOW TO BUILD A BRICK & CEDAR FENCE

Install the Footings

Measure and mark the fence line with stakes and mason's string.

Determine the center of each pillar location along the fence line. To space the pillars at 96" edge to edge, drop a plumb bob 12" in from the end of the fence line, and then every 116". Place a stake at each pillar location.

Outline 16 × 20" pillar footings at each location, then dig the trenches and pour the footings. Let the footings cure for two days.

Lay the First Course

On a flat work surface, lay out a row of bricks, spaced ⅜" apart. Mark the identical spacing on a 2 × 2 to create a story pole.

Dry-lay the first course of five bricks—center them on the footing, leaving ⅜" spaces between them. Mark reference lines around the bricks with chalk.

Set the bricks aside and trowel a ⅜"-layer of mortar inside the reference lines. Set a brick into the mortar, with the end aligned with the reference lines. Set a level on top of the brick, then tap the brick with the trowel handle until it's level.

- Tools & materials for pouring footings
- Tape measure
- Level
- Plumb bob
- Wheelbarrow or mixing box
- Mason's trowel
- Jointing tool
- Aviation snips
- Drill
- Circular saw
- Hammer
- Jig saw
- Standard modular bricks (4 × 2⅔ × 8", 130 per pillar)
- 2 × 2 lumber, 10 ft.
- Chalk
- Type N mortar mix

- ¼" wooden dowel & vegetable oil
- ¼" wire mesh
- Capstone or concrete cap
- ⅜"-thick wood scraps
- 2 × 6 corrosion-resistant fence brackets (6 per bay)
- 1¼" countersink concrete screws
- Concrete drill bit
- Pressure-treated, cedar, or redwood lumber:
  - 1 × 6, 8 ft. (16 per bay)
  - 2 × 6, 8 ft. (3 per bay)
- 1½" corrosion-resistant deck screws
- 1½" finish nails (3)
- 96"-length of flexible ¼" PVC pipe

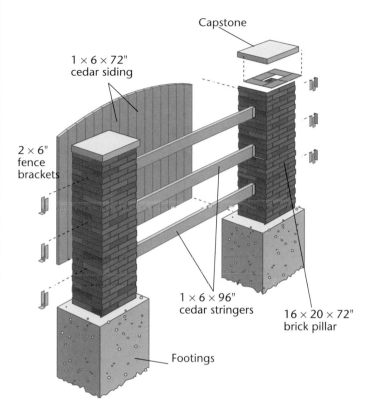

Capstone

1 × 6 × 72" cedar siding

2 × 6" fence brackets

1 × 6 × 96" cedar stringers

16 × 20 × 72" brick pillar

Footings

Set the rest of the bricks in the mortar, buttering the mating ends with mortar. Use the reference lines to keep the bricks aligned, and make sure they are plumb and level.

Cutting List

Each 96" bay requires:

Part	Type	Size	Number
Stringers	2 × 6	96"	3
Siding	1 × 6	72"	16

1 Pour footings that are 4" longer and wider than the pillars on each side. This project calls for 16 × 20" footings.

2 Trowel a bed of mortar inside the reference lines and lay the first course. Create a weep hole in the mortar with a dowel to ensure the drainage of any moisture that seeps into the pillar.

3 Lay each new course so the bricks overlap the joints of the previous course. Use a jointing tool after every five courses to smooth the firm mortar joints.

4 Lay the final course over a bed of mortar and wire mesh, with an additional block added to the center. Fill the joints with mortar, and work them with a jointing tool as soon as they become firm.

5 Spread a ½"-thick bed of mortar on top of the pillar, and center the cap, using the reference lines.

Use a pencil or dowel coated with vegetable oil to create a weep hole in the mortar of the first course of bricks, so that any moisture that seeps into the pillar will drain away.

Lay the Subsequent Courses

Lay the second course, rotating the pattern 180°, so the joints of the first course are overlapped by the bricks of the second course.

Lay the subsequent courses, rotating the pattern 180° with each course. Use the story pole and a level to check the faces of the pillar after every other course. Use the story pole after every few courses to make sure the mortar joints are consistent.

After every fourth course, cut a strip of ¼" wire mesh and place it over a thin bed of mortar. Add another thin bed of mortar on top of the mesh, then add the next course of brick.

After every five courses, use a jointing tool to smooth the joints when they have hardened enough to resist minimal finger pressure.

Lay the Final Course

For the final course, lay the bricks over a bed of mortar and wire mesh. After placing the first two bricks, add an extra brick in the center of the course. Lay the remainder of the bricks to fit around it.

Fill the remaining joints, and work them with the jointing tool as soon as they become firm.

Build the next pillars in the same way as the first. Use the story pole to maintain identical dimensions and a 96" length of 2 × 2 to keep the spacing between pillars consistent.

Install the Top Cap

Select a capstone 3" longer and wider than the top of the pillar. Mark reference lines on the bottom of the capstone to help you center it.

Spread a ½"-thick bed of mortar on top of the pillar. Center the capstone on the pillar, using the reference lines. Strike the mortar joint under the cap so it's flush with the pillar. If mortar squeezes out of the joints, press ⅜"-thick wood scraps into the mortar at each corner to support the cap. Remove the scraps after 24 hours and fill the gaps with mortar.

Attach the Stringers

On the inner face of each pillar (the face perpendicular to the fence line), measure down from the top and use chalk to mark at 18", 36", and 60".

At each mark, measure in 6¾" from the outside face of the pillar and mark with the chalk. Position a 2 × 6 fence bracket at the point where the reference marks intersect. Mark the screw holes on the pillar face, two or three per bracket.

Drill 1¾"-deep embedment holes at each mark, using the bit provided with the concrete screws. The hole must be ¼" deeper than the length of the screw.

6 Attach 2 × 6 fence brackets to the pillars, using 1¼" countersink concrete screws.

Align the fence bracket screw holes with the embedment holes, and drive the 1¼" concrete screws into the pillar. Repeat for each pillar, attaching three fence brackets on each side of each line pillar.

Measure the distance from a fence bracket of the first pillar to the corresponding fence bracket of the next to determine the exact length of the stringers. If necessary, mark and then cut a cedar 2 × 6 to length, using a circular saw.

Insert a 2 × 6 stringer into a pair of fence brackets and attach it with 1½" corrosion-resistant screws. Repeat for each stringer.

Cut the Section Arch

Cut 1" off the ends of the cedar 1 × 6s to create a square edge.

On a large, flat surface, such as a driveway, lay out sixteen 1 × 6s, with approximately ½" of space between them and the cut ends flush.

On the two end boards, measure up from the bottom and mark 64". Tack a 1½" finish nail into each mark, 2" from the edge of the board.

Draw a line connecting the nails. Measure and mark the center (48" from the edge in our project). At the center, mark a point 6" above the original line. This mark indicates the height of the arch.

Place a 96"-long piece of flexible PVC piping against the two nails. At the mid-point, bend the PVC pipe until it meets the height mark. Tack a 1½" finish nail behind the PVC pipe to hold it in place, then trace along the PVC pipe to form the arch. Cut the arch, using a jig saw to cut along the marked line.

Attach the Siding

Run a mason's string 2" above the bottom of the fence line as a guide.

Attach the siding to the stringers, using 1½" galvanized deck screws. Maintain a 2" gap at the bottom of the fence, and make sure the boards are plumb. Use ½" scraps of wood as spacing guides between boards.

Repeat for each section of fence.

7 Align cedar slats for a 96" section, and tack two nails on opposite sides, 64" from the bottom. Deflect a piece of PVC pipe against the nails, 6" up from the middle, and trace the arch.

8 Attach the cedar slats to the stringers with 1½" corrosion-resistant deck screws. Maintain their order to properly form the arch top.

Stone & Rail Fence

This 36"-tall, rustic stone-and-rail fence is constructed in much the same way as the brick and cedar fence, but with stone rather than brick and simple 2 × 4 rails rather than siding. Each pillar requires a footing that extends 6" beyond its base in all directions. Carefully plan the layout and sort the stones before you begin setting the stone. If necessary, use a stone cutter's chisel and a maul to trim stones or cut them to size.

HOW TO BUILD A STONE & RAIL FENCE

Dry-lay the First Course

Plot the fence line with stakes and mason's string (pages 18 to 19). For 72" bays between 24 × 24" pillars, measure and mark 18" in from the end of the fence line and then every 96" on-center.

Outline, dig, and pour 36 × 36" concrete footings. Let the concrete cure for two days.

Sort individual stones by size and shape. Set aside suitable tie stones for corners and the largest stones for the base.

Dry-lay the outside stones in the first course to form a 24 × 24" base centered on the footing.

Use chalk to trace a reference outline on the footing around the stones, then set them aside.

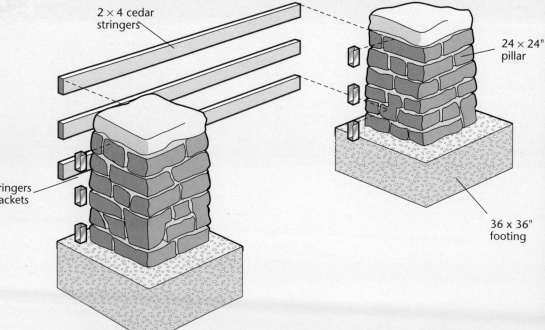

2 × 4 cedar stringers

24 × 24" pillar

Stringers brackets

36 × 36" footing

Mortar the First Course

Trowel a 1"-thick bed of mortar inside the reference outline, then place the stones in the mortar, in the same positions as in the dry-run. Fill in the center with small stones and mortar. Leave the center slightly lower than the outer stones. Pack mortar between the outer stones, recessing it roughly 1".

Lay More Courses & Tool the Joints

Set each subsequent course of stone in a bed of mortar laid over the preceding course, staggering the vertical joints. On every other course, place tie stones that extend into the pillar center. Use wood shims to support large stones until the mortar sets. Build each pillar 36" tall, using a level to check for plumb.

When the mortar sets enough to resist light finger pressure, smooth the joints with a jointing tool. Keep the mortar 1" back from the stone faces. Remove any shims and fill the holes with mortar. Remove dry spattered mortar with a dry, stiff-bristle brush.

Lay Top Cap & Attach the Stringers

Lay a 1"-thick bed of mortar on the pillar top and place the capstones. Smooth the joints. Mist with water regularly for one week, as the mortar cures.

On the inner face of each pillar, measure up from the footing and mark with chalk 12", 21", and 30". At each mark, measure in 6" from the outside face of the pillar and mark, then line up the top and side edges of a 2 × 4 fence bracket where these two marks intersect. Mark the screw holes on the pillar, then drill a 1½"-deep embedment hole at each mark.

Align the bracket screw holes with the embedment holes, and attach with the 1¼" countersink concrete screws. Repeat for each bracket. Measure the distance from a fence bracket on one pillar to the corresponding bracket on the next for the stringer size. Mark and cut stringers to size. Paint, stain, or seal each stringer, and allow to dry. Insert stringers into the fence brackets and attach them, using 1½" corrosion-resistant screws.

1 Spread a 1"-thick bed of mortar on top of the footing, and beginning stacking the stones inside the pillar outline. Fill gaps between stones with mortar and spread a bed of mortar over the first-course stones.

2 Build up courses of stones, checking with a level and adding or subtracting mortar as you go to keep each course level. Fill gaps between stones and smooth with a jointing tool.

3 Spread a 1"-thick bed of mortar on the top course of stones and set the cap block into the mortar. Clean off excess mortar and smooth out the mortar joints with a jointing tool. Attach fence rail hangers and fence rails as described.

TOOLS & MATERIALS

- Tape measure
- Level
- Wheelbarrow or mixing box
- Mason's trowel
- Jointing tool
- Stone cutter's chisel & maul
- Stiff-bristle brush
- Drill
- Paintbrush & roller
- Type M mortar

- Stones of various shapes and sizes
- Wood shims
- Fence brackets (6 per bay)
- 1¼" countersink concrete screws
- Concrete drill bit
- Rough-cut cedar 2 × 4s, 8 ft. (3 per bay)
- Paint, stain, or sealer
- 1½" corrosion-resistant deck screws

Cedar & Copper Fence

This cedar & copper fence can wear many faces: by staining the lumber and sealing the copper, you can give it a tailored, contemporary look; by leaving the lumber and copper unfinished, you can create a weathered, rustic look. Or, by painting the lumber and sealing the copper to keep it bright, you can create a fresh, crisp look.

Regardless of the finish you choose, this clever combination of cedar and copper pipe produces a durable fence with an interesting appearance. It provides security with-

out completely compromising your view—in fact, we first saw a fence similar to this separating a swimming pool from a wildlife area.

The design was perfect for that situation: the height and the vertical nature of the fence made it difficult to breach, but the openness preserved the natural view beyond the fence line. Of course, regulations regarding fences around swimming pools vary by municipality, so it's especially important to check local building codes before planning such a fence.

HOW TO BUILD A CEDAR & COPPER FENCE

Set the Posts & Prepare the Materials

Mark the fence line with stakes and mason's string.

Calculate the post spacing based on the contour of the land along the fence line and mark the post locations. Set the posts, and adjust each post so that it is 66" above ground level.

Cut the lumber as described in the cutting list at right. Paint, stain, or seal all the pieces.

Make the Pipe Holders

Make a storyboard for the pipe spacing: On the edge of a 1 × 2, make a mark every 4"—you'll have a total of 22 marks.

For each bay, you'll need one 1 × 3 holder for the bottom of the fence and one 2 × 2 holder for the top. Use a combination square to draw a center line along the length of each pipe holder. Line up the storyboard along the center line and transfer the marks.

Drill a ½" hole at each mark, using a drill and spade bit. To keep the boards from splitting out, place the 2 × 2 over a piece of scrap lumber as you drill.

Calculate the number of pipes necessary for your fence line, and cut the appropriate number of 55" pieces of ½" copper pipe, using a tubing cutter or hacksaw.

Attach the Stringer Supports

At the first post, mark a level line across the inside face of the post, 2" from the ground. Align a 2 × 4 stringer support above that line and fasten it to the post with 2½" corrosion-resistant deck screws.

Using a chalk line and line level, mark a level position on the opposite post. Use a framing square to transfer that mark to the inside face of the post, then fasten a stringer support to that post.

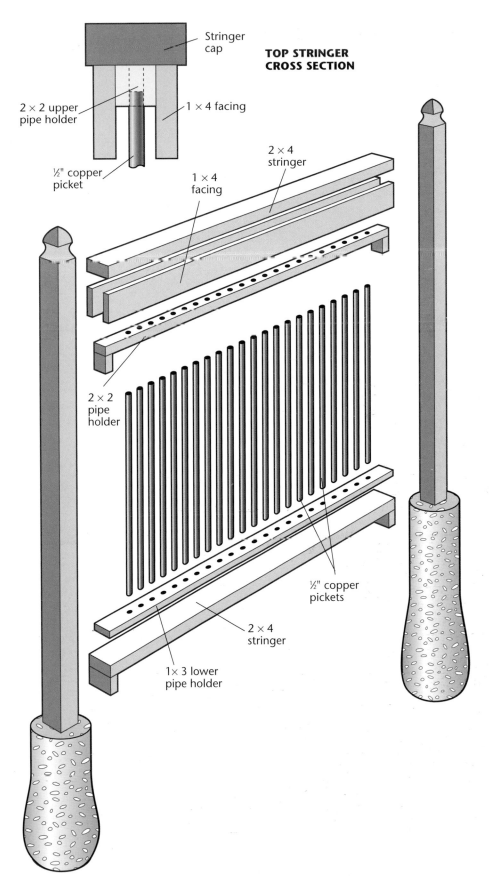

TOP STRINGER CROSS SECTION

Stringer cap

2 × 2 upper pipe holder

1 × 4 facing

½" copper picket

1 × 4 facing

2 × 4 stringer

2 × 2 pipe holder

½" copper pickets

2 × 4 stringer

1 × 3 lower pipe holder

Install the Lower Stringer & Pipe Support

Set a 2 × 4 on top of the stringer supports and drive 2½" corrosion-resistant deck screws at an angle, through the stringer and support, and into the post.

Set a 1 × 3 pipe holder in place, centered on top of the stringer. Drive 2" corrosion-resistant deck screws through the pipe holder and down into the stringer. Add screws between every other pair of holes in the 1 × 3.

Install the Upper Pipe Holder

Mark a level line on the inside face of the post, 3" down from the flare of the post. Measure the distance between the top of the lower stringer and the bottom of the upper stringer support. Transfer that measurement to the inside face of the opposite post and draw a level line.

On each post, align a stringer support below the mark and fasten it to the post with 2½" corrosion-resistant deck screws.

Set a 2 × 2 pipe holder on top of the stringer supports and drive 2½" corrosion-resistant deck screws at an angle through the support and into the post.

Place the Pipes & Add the Facings

Working from above the upper pipe holder, insert a pipe into each hole and settle it into the corresponding hole in the bottom.

Position a 1 × 4 facing on the one side of the pipe holder, flush with the top of the 2 × 2. Fasten the 1 × 4 in place, using 2" corrosion-resistant deck screws. Add a second facing on the other side of the fence.

Center a 2 × 4 stringer on top of the structure; secure it with 2½" corrosion-resistant deck screws.

Note: Built one bay at a time as described, this design can accommodate a slight slope. If you have a more radical slope to deal with, refer to pages 14 to 17 for further information.

TOOLS & MATERIALS

- Tools & materials for setting posts
- Paintbrush & roller
- Combination square
- Drill & spade bit
- Tubing cutter or hacksaw
- Chalk line
- Line level
- Framing square
- Paint, stain, or sealer
- Pressure treated, cedar, or redwood lumber:

- 1 × 2, 8 ft. (1 per bay)
- 1 × 3, 8 ft. (1 per bay)
- 2 × 2, 8 ft. (1 per bay)
- 2 × 4, 8 ft. (2 per bay)
- 1 × 4, 8 ft. (2 per bay)
- ½" copper pipe, 10 ft. (11 per bay)
- 2½" galvanized deck screws
- 2" galvanized deck screws
- Stakes & mason's string

HOW TO BUILD A CEDAR & COPPER FENCE

1 Cut the lumber, then paint, stain or seal the pieces. Mark the fence line and set the posts.

2 Mark 4" on center spacing on the edge of a 1 × 2. Mark a center line on the pipe holder lumber, then transfer the spacing marks. Drill ½" holes, using a drill and spade bit.

3 Mark a level line and then attach a stringer support on the inside face of each post.

4 Fasten the stringers to the posts, then center the lower pipe holder on top of the stringer. Drive screws down through the 1 × 3 and into the stringer.

5 Mark positions for the upper stringer supports and attach them to the inside faces of the posts. Add the upper pipe supports and secure them, using 2½" corrosion-resistant deck screws.

6 Insert the pipes into the holes in the upper pipe holder and settle them into the corresponding holes in the lower pipe holder. Add 1 × 4 facings, then top the structure with a 2 × 4 stringer.

Shadow Box Fence

Garden tools and implements seem to multiply in the night. Many of today's tools are attractive as well as functional—rather than hiding them in a garage or shed, why not use them to accessorize a fence bay?

HOW TO BUILD A SHADOW BOX

Prepare the Materials & Install the Vertical Supports

Determine the number and location of the vertical supports. Measure the distance between the stringers in those locations, and cut 2 × 4s to length.

Determine the locations of the shelves and measure the distance between the vertical supports in those locations. Cut 1 × 4s to length.

Paint, stain, or seal the lumber to match or complement the fence. If you like the look shown here, paint the sections of the fence siding as well.

Position the vertical supports and secure them to the stringers with pairs of angle irons and 1" corrosion-resistant deck screws.

Prepare the Shelves

Measure the diameter of your pots, just below the edge of the rim. Use a compass to draw appropriately-sized, evenly-spaced circles across one of the shelves. Cut out the circles, using a jig saw.

Attach decorative molding to the front edge of one shelf, using exterior wood glue and corrosion-resistant finish nails.

Drill four evenly-spaced holes

1 Secure the vertical supports with pairs of angle irons and 1" corrosion-resistant deck screws.

TOOLS & MATERIALS

- Tape measure
- Circular saw
- Paintbrushes & roller
- Drill
- Compass
- Jig saw
- Hammer
- 1 × 4 lumber
- Paint, stain, or sealer
- 1" corrosion-resistant deck screws
- Angle irons, 4 for each support or shelf
- 2" corrosion-resistant deck screws
- Exterior wood glue
- Decorative molding
- Corrosion-resistant finish nails
- Decorative knobs or pegs (4)
- Clay pots
- Gardening tools
- Herbs, annuals, trailing vines

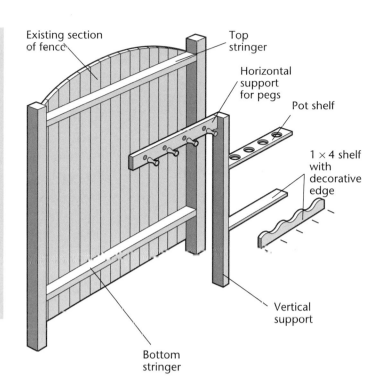

Existing section of fence

Top stringer

Horizontal support for pegs

Pot shelf

1 × 4 shelf with decorative edge

Vertical support

Bottom stringer

across a horizontal support, using a bit that matches the size of the stems on your knobs or pegs.

Screw in the knobs or secure the pegs with exterior wood glue.

Install the Shelves

Install the horizontal supports, using 2" corrosion-resistant deck screws.

Position the shelves according to your planned layout, and secure them with pairs of angle irons and 1" corrosion-resistant deck screws.

Add Accessories

Add pots of herbs or annuals. Hang gardening tools from the pegs. If you want to get even more creative, you could install a brass hook on a vertical support to hold a gardening hat or apron. It might also be fun to put a mirror behind the pot holder. Have a mirror cut to fit that section, seal the back with polyurethane, and fasten it with construction adhesive.

2 Cut holes for pots in one 1 × 4, add decorative molding to another, and add knobs to a third.

3 Drive 2" corrosion-resistant deck screws through the face of the horizontal support and into the siding.

4 Add accessories and embellishments as desired.

Framed Fence Openings

Framing an opening into a broad expanse of solid fence can create a lively view or let you display a decorative piece. To frame an opening:

HOW TO BUILD A FRAMED OPENING FENCE

Mark the Opening

Measure the item to be framed into the fence or decide on the dimensions of the opening.

Select the location for the opening. Consider the direction of the sun if you're framing in a piece of stained glass or the view beyond the fence if you're planning a simple window.

Use a level and a framing square to mark the opening on the siding of the fence.

Cut an Opening in the Siding

Drill a hole in one corner of the opening, then slip the blade of a jig saw or reciprocating saw into that hole and cut along the marked lines.

Add the Frame

Measure the opening. To calculate the lengths for the top and bottom pieces of the frame, add 7" to the width of the opening. Mark and cut four pieces of 1 × 4 lumber to this length.

TOOLS & MATERIALS

- Tape measure
- Level
- Framing square
- Drill
- Jig saw or reciprocating saw
- Paintbrushes & roller
- Circular saw
- Spring clamps
- Hammer
- Tack hammer
- Display piece
- 1 × 4 lumber
- Paint, stain, or sealer
- 2¼" corrosion-resistant deck screws
- 1 × 1 lumber
- Finish nails

For the four side pieces, mark and cut 1 × 4 lumber to match the height of the opening exactly.

Paint, stain, or seal the frame pieces to match or complement the fence. Allow to dry thoroughly.

Carefully align the side pieces with the edge of the opening and clamp them in place. Drill evenly-spaced pilot holes, then drive 2¼" corrosion-resistant deck screws through the trim and siding and into the trim on the back side of the fence. Repeat this procedure with the top and bottom pieces.

Position the Display Piece & Add Trim

Measure the display piece and determine how it will sit within the opening. Cut 1 × 1s to fit around the piece, framing both the front and back.

On the back side of the opening, drill pilot holes and drive finish nails through the 1 × 1s and into the frame pieces.

Position the display piece and add the trim on the front side. Carefully nail the trim in place, using finish nails and a tack hammer.

1 Determine measurements and draw an opening on the siding of the fence, using a framing square and a level. Make certain the opening is square, plumb, and properly positioned.

2 Drill a pilot hole in one corner of the outline. Insert the blade of a jig saw and cut along the marked lines.

3 Sandwich the opening with 1 × 4 trim and clamp the trim in place. Drill pilot holes and drive 2¼" corrosion-resistant deck screws through the trim and siding.

4 Position the first set of trim pieces and secure them with finish nails. Position the display piece and the second set of trim. Carefully nail the trim in place, using a tack hammer and finish nails.

Garden Walls

W all. The word itself evokes visions of a barrier—tall, solid, and imposing. But in your yard, walls can't be defined in such a limited way. Landscape walls serve many purposes: they can define the property boundaries, separate living areas within the yard, and screen off unpleasant views or utility spaces.

With a temporary wall, you can create privacy and intimacy without building a permanent structure. On the other hand, if you want permanence, little could be more durable than masonry walls. Masonry walls, such as glass block, concrete block, stone or stone veneer, and can introduce new textures and patterns into your landscape.

Living walls are another striking option. In some spots, a hedge might be just the thing to create a dense visual screen, diffuse wind, or absorb noise. Trellis walls, such as the post and wire trellis or the framed trellis wall, provide beautiful backdrops for your favorite vines or lush border gardens.

Using simple building techniques, the projects in this chapter offer a wide variety of choices for practical, visually appealing walls. Properly constructed, the walls you build should last decades with little maintenance.

IN THIS CHAPTER:

Types of Walls

Before deciding what style of wall you want to build, take a close look at what purpose you want the wall to serve. Walls, in contrast to fences, do not necessarily enclose an area. But like fences, they can partially or completely block a view, define your property lines, or provide privacy. They can also prevent or direct movement between two areas.

And in smaller lengths, some structures you may not think of as walls, such as trellises and arbors, can serve as backdrops to your landscape.

If you'd like to define your yard but retain a natural-looking landscape, a tall, dense hedge may be the best choice. On the other hand, if you need to provide privacy and security, mortared block may be the most effective solution.

Generally, the purpose for your wall will dictate its size, but consider its setting and the size of your lot when you're deciding on dimensions. Local codes often set regulations regarding size, as well as acceptable materials, footings and other reinforcements, and bulding permits. Always check local building codes before beginning any building or landscaping project.

Temporary Walls

Painted canvas draped over copper pipe makes an inexpensive, easily-stored alternative to a fixed structure.

Living Walls

Whether spaced closely in a hedge or trained to grow over a trellis, plants create living walls that soften the texture of a landscape.

• Post & Wire Trellis
• Wall of Arbors
• Hedges
• Framed Trellis Wall

Block Walls

Concrete or glass, blocks produce sturdy, durable walls that are surprisingly easy to build. Low block walls are used mostly for effect, but full-size mortared block walls also provide excellent security.

• Mortarless Block Wall
• Mortared Block Wall
• Glass Block Wall

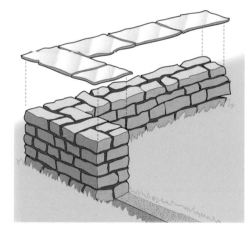

Stone Walls

With or without mortar, stone walls lend a sense of permanence to a landscape. Though more expensive and time-consuming to build than other types of walls, stone walls stand for decades as testimony to the builder's patience and craftmanship.

• Dry Stone Wall
• Mortared Stone Wall

Temporary Wall

Not everyone wants permanent walls or fences. But even if you want to preserve a view or prefer the look of a wide-open landscape, there may be times when you'd like a little more privacy. A temporary wall can create a special setting for an intimate dinner, provide some late afternoon shade on a deck or patio, or screen a sunbather from view.

For this project, we painted canvas and then stretched it across a frame made of copper pipe and fittings. To create texture, we used two colors of paint and a specialty roller. These rollers, which come with complete instructions, are widely available.

Hinge extensions—similar to the ones used for the copper gate—allow the wall to be folded for storage. Review the instructions and photos for the copper gate project before beginning this one.

HOW TO BUILD A TEMPORARY WALL

Construct the Frames

Measure and mark the pipe for the first section of the wall, according to the diagram at right.

Cut the copper pipe to length, using a tubing cutter. Sand the ends of all the pipes with emery cloth, and scour the insides of the fittings with a wire brush. Apply flux to all the mating surfaces.

Dry-fit the pieces of the frame. Crimp the fittings with pliers and rotate the pipes within to lock assembly together. Exception: Don't crimp the lower horizontal brace.

Solder joints, starting at the bottom and working up. Do not solder the lower horizontal brace to the frame.

Note: The end frames are identical. The center frame has two hinge sides with hinge elbows pointing up instead of down. Also, Lengths of E & C (facing page) are reversed to offset mating hinges.

If you have the time and talent, you can stencil a trompe l'oeil on the canvas.

TOOLS & MATERIALS

- Tape measure
- Tubing cutter
- ¾" wire fitting and pipe brush
- Propane torch
- Caulk gun
- Spring clamps
- Locking pliers
- Drill
- Pop rivet gun
- ¾" copper pipe, 60 ft.
- ¾" copper tees (20)
- ¾" copper end caps (12)

- ¾" copper 90° elbows (14)
- ⅝ × ¾" brass flange bearings (8)
- Emery cloth
- Flux & flux brush
- Solder
- Canvas, 5 yds.
- Latex paint
- Stencils
- Silicone caulk
- Steel pop rivets (24)
- Leather gloves
- Eye protection

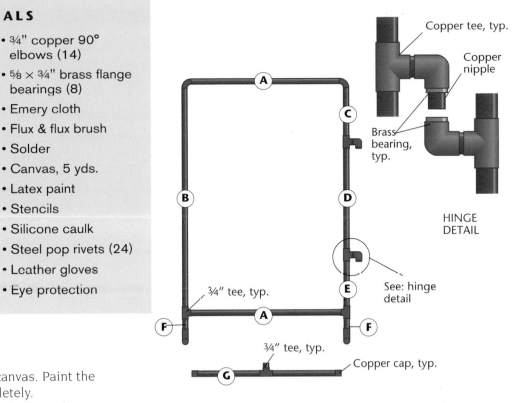

Copper tee, typ.

Copper nipple

Brass bearing, typ.

¾" tee, typ.

See: hinge detail

¾" tee, typ.

Copper cap, typ.

HINGE DETAIL

Construct the Canvas

Cut three 68" lengths of canvas. Paint the canvas, and let it dry completely.

Run a bead of silicone caulk along the center of the top crosspiece of the first frame. Center the canvas within the frame and press it into the bead of caulk; clamp the fabric in place until the caulk dries. Wrap the fabric around the crosspiece.

Run a bead of caulk along the lower crosspiece and clamp the canvas in place. When the caulk is dry, use a pair of locking pliers to turn the crosspiece within the fittings. Turn the pipe until the canvas is wrapped around the pipe and the fabric is taut across the frame.

Drill four evenly spaced pilot holes across each crosspiece. Secure the canvas to the pipe, using a pop rivet gun and steel pop rivets.

Cutting List
(totals for three 5 ft. frames)

Key	Part	Size	Number
A	Horizontal braces	38½"	6
B	Vertical braces	54¼"	2
C	Hinge sides braces	13½"	4
D	Middle hinge side brace	24¾"	4
E	Hinge sides braces	14½"	4
F	Legs	3½"	6
G	Feet	9¾"	12
H	Canvas	38¼" × 68"	3

1 Mark and cut the copper pipe, then clean and flux the pipe and fittings. Assemble and solder the frames. Do not solder the lower crosspiece.

2 Paint strips of canvas and let them dry. Secure the canvas to the frame with silicone caulk and pop rivets.

Post & Wire Trellis

Successful gardens often seem to be studies in contrast. Great gardeners blend and contrast plant forms, colors, and textures, using each to its greatest advantage. Texture is an important element of this design equation.

To create the illusion of depth in a shallow planting bed, designers recommend using a vertical display of fine-textured foliage as a backdrop for several plants with large, coarse leaves. Although many trellises are designed to support a riot of flowers or a rambunctious layer of foliage, few provide an adequate showcase for the type of delicate texture required in this situation.

It may sound like a big challenge to build a trellis that accomplishes this mission, matches the average person's construction abilities, and falls within a reasonable budget, but this project is remarkably simple. By topping cedar posts with decorative finials and stringing a lattice of plastic-coated wire between them, you can create a trellis that would be ideal for many garden settings.

The best plants for this trellis are twining climbers with small leaves. Among annual vines you can try sweet pea or cardinal climber. Good perennial vines include trumpet creeper, English ivy, and winter creeper. You can put your climbers in the ground or select a variety that thrives in planters or pots. Be sure, however, that the plants you choose are well-suited to the light exposure they'll receive.

TOOLS & MATERIALS

- Tape measure
- Posthole digger or power auger
- Carpenter's level
- Drill
- Stakes & mason's string
- Circular saw
- Wheelbarrow
- Trowel
- Hammer
- Wood sealer
- Pea gravel
- Quick-setting concrete mix

- 8 ft. cedar 4 × 4s (2)
- Scrap 2 × 4s
- Deck post finials (2)
- 2 × 3 corrosion-resistant fence brackets (4)
- 8 ft. cedar 2 × 4s (2)
- 1", 1½" fence bracket screws
- 1½" screw eyes
- Plastic-coated wire or clothesline
- Small corrosion-resistant finish nails
- Combination square
- Folding stick ruler

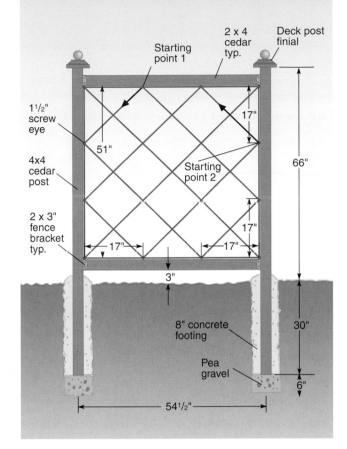

HOW TO BUILD A POST & WIRE TRELLIS

Prepare Posts, Dig Holes

Apply wood sealer to the bottom 3ft. of each post and let dry. For extra protection, let the bottom of the post soak in wood sealer overnight.

At the chosen site, mark the posthole locations by setting two wooden stakes in the ground, 54½" apart.

Dig your postholes to 36". If you intend to use concrete, widen the postholes at the bottoms and keep the hole tops narrow with forming collars.

Set the first post into a hole. Take a carpenter's level and make sure the post is plumb on two adjacent sides.

When the post is plumb, use stakes and scrap pieces of 2 × 4 to brace it in position. Repeat the process for the other post.

When both posts are plumb and braced, use a mason's string to make certain the tops and sides are aligned. Adjust as necessary.

1 Align, space, plumb and brace your posts according to Setting Posts on page 22.

2 While concrete lends greater stability to tall structures than dirt and gravel, it's best used with pressure treated wood. Untreated and topically treated posts will rot faster in concrete.

Set Posts

Brace and align the posts plumb on six inches of pea gravel as you would for a fence. Use a spacing template to maintain a 51" in. gap between facing sides of the posts. Set a level on a straight 2 × 4 across the post tops to level.

Set the posts in concrete or packed soil and gravel. Concrete makes a more stable base for pressure treated posts. Natural cedar will rot sooner in concrete footings.

Check the post one more time to make sure it's plumb and properly aligned.

With a trowel, form the wet concrete into a gentle mound around the base of the post.

Repeat the process for the other post, taking care that it's plumb and aligned with the first post.

Let the concrete set for one to two hours.

Install the Finials

Set a decorative deck post finial on top of each post. Drill two pilot holes on each side and secure the finials with small corrosion-resistant finish nails.

Install the Stringers

Draw a mason's string between the posts three inches up from the grade and level it with a line level. Transfer the line crossings to the inside faces of the posts with a combination square and pencil.

Center fence brackets on your posts so they'll hold the stringer bottoms at your lines. Attach with bracket screws.

Use a stick rule to measure most of the distance between the insides of the brackets, then make up the difference with a tape measure. Cut the bottom stringer to this length. Fasten it in the brackets with bracket screws.

Measure and mark each post 51 inches up from the stringer tops. Align, center and attach upper fence brackets to these marks as you did the bottom brackets. Cut and fasten the upper stringer.

3 On top of each post, set a decorative deck finial. Drill pilot holes and secure the finials with small corrosion-resistant finish nails.

4 Attach the fence brackets 3" from the bottoms of the posts, using sheet metal screws.

5 Run wire diagonally between the screw eyes on the posts and stringers.

Install the Screw Eyes & String the Wire

Starting in one corner where a stringer meets a post, make a mark on the inside edge of the stringer, 17" from the corner. Next, mark the inside face of the post, 17" from the corner. Repeat the process for the remaining three corners.

Drill pilot holes and attach screw eyes centered on the post or stringer at each of the marked locations.

Knot plastic-coated wire or clothesline on the eye at starting point 1 and complete indicated rectangle. Wire indicated rectangle from starting point 2. Finish by wiring the diagonals and the edges.

VARIATION: SIMPLE TRELLIS PLAN

1. You can build an easier, less decorative version of the Post & Wire Trellis without the stringers and the crosshatch wire layout. Start by following the directions for Steps A through C.

2. Measuring 1" from the inside tops of the posts, mark the location of the first screw eye. Then continue marking screw eye locations every 8" down the post, putting the last mark a few inches off the ground. Repeat the process for the other post.

3. Drill pilot holes and install the screw eyes, twisting them so that the "eyes" are parallel to the ground, not at right angles to it.

4. Attach the plastic-coated wire with a secure knot to one of the top screw eyes. Then feed the wire through the screw eye on the opposite side, then down through the screw eye directly below.

5. Pull the wire across to the second screw eye down on the opposite side, feeding it through and down to the screw eye directly below. Keep the wire as taut as possible at every run.

6. Continue this process until you reach the final screw eye, and then knot the wire securely.

Hanging Baskets Addition

1. To make use of the outside or front edge of the posts, install decorative brackets for hanging plants. Position brackets along the side or front of the post as desired, centered along the post. Mark the screw holes and drill pilot holes. Each post should accommodate at least two brackets.

2. Attach brackets with the screws supplied, and hang planter baskets.

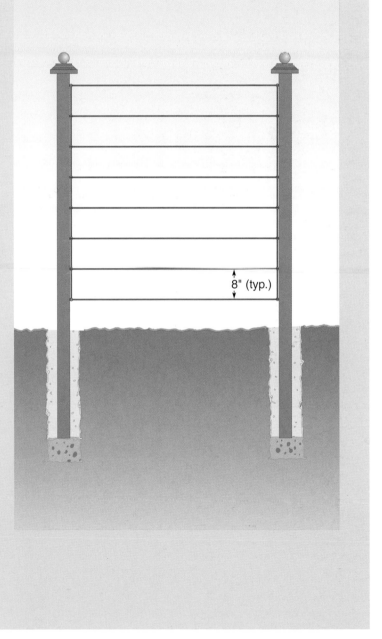

8" (typ.)

Wall of Arbors

Rather than acting as a barrier, this wall of arbors welcomes visitors with open arms. Planted with roses or flowering vines, it creates a luxurious, ornamental accent to your yard or garden.

Gracefully connected side-by-side, these arched arbors could, in addition to providing an accent to your yard, mark a property line or define an outdoor living space. And with well chosen plantings, they can either partially screen out or enhance a view, depending on your preferences.

Copper plumbing materials go together much like children's construction toys, so these arbors are fun to build. If you're new to soldering, this is a good project to learn on—the size is manageable and the joints don't have to be absolutely watertight. Just work carefully and remember that if you don't get the joints right the first time, the materials aren't wasted. You can reheat the solder, pop off and clean the fittings, and start again. You do, however, have to be precise about the alignment of certain pieces so the arbors fit together well when you connect them to one another.

TOOLS & MATERIALS

- Tape measure
- Tubing cutter
- Drill/driver
- Round file (optional)
- Propane torch
- Hand maul
- Plywood scraps, at least 10 × 40" (2)
- 6 to 8" pieces of ⅜" dowel (4)
- 1 × 2s, at least 46" long (2)
- 1" deck screws (8)
- Wood glue
- ½" copper pipe (5 10-ft. sticks per arbor)
- ½" copper tees (20 per arbor)
- ½" copper 45° elbows (4 per arbor)
- ½" copper 90° elbows (2 per arbor)
- Emery cloth or nylon scouring pad
- ¾" Wire fitting and pipe brush
- Flux & flux brush
- Solder
- #3 rebar, 36" sections (2 per arbor)
- Stakes & string
- Leather gloves
- Eye protection
- Pliers
- Carpenter's square

HOW TO BUILD A WALL OF ARBORS

Cut the Pipe & Build a Support Jig

Measure, mark and cut copper pipe according to cutting list below right. Do not cut four of the 19½" pieces for each arbor.

To build a support jig, start with two scraps of plywood at least 10" wide and 35 to 40" long. Draw a line down the center of each piece of plywood, then drill two ⅜" holes, 20" apart along the line. Glue a 6 to 8" piece of dowel into each hole. On each of two 1 × 2s, draw a pair of marks 42½" apart. Square the 1 × 2s with the lines on the plywood and secure with 1" screws.

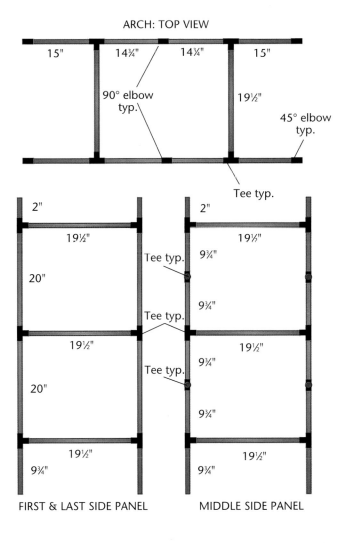

ARCH: TOP VIEW

FIRST & LAST SIDE PANEL   MIDDLE SIDE PANEL

1 Make a support jig: attach pieces of dowel to scraps of plywood, then use 1 × 2s as spacers to set the distance between the sides of the jig.

Cutting List

For each arbor, you need ½" copper pipe in these lengths:

Length	Quantity
15"	4
14¾"	4
2"	4
20"	4*
19½"	12
9¾"	12 or 20**

* For first and last Arbor

** 12 for first and last Arbor,
20 for each intermediate arbor

2 Dry fit the leg assemblies: alternate pipe and tees to form the legs, then add horizontal supports.

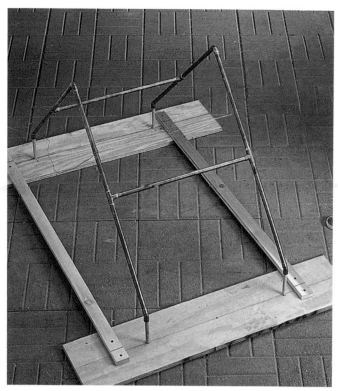

3 Using 90° elbows, pipe, and tees, build the arch assemblies. Connect the arches with horizontal braces and tees. Leave 45-degree elbows unsoldered.

4 Position the first arbor, and press its legs into the ground to mark their positions. At two opposite corners, drive 36" pieces of rebar 18" into the ground. Settle the arbor over the rebar.

5 Position and anchor the second arbor. Add horizontal braces, then solder them into position.

Prep and Flux Pipe Ends and Fittings as You Assemble the Arbors

Construct the Leg Assemblies

Slide a 9¾" length of pipe over the first dowel, add a tee, then alternate pipe and tees as indicated on the drawing on page 83.

Slide a 9¾" length of pipe over the second dowel, then alternate tees and pipe as indicated.

Fit 19½" lengths of pipe between pairs of tees to form horizontal supports. Insert the 2" pipe stubs in the top tees.

Repeat numbers 1 through 3 to construct a leg assembly for the other side of the arbor. Note that the outside leg assembly at end arbors uses longer pipe sections and fewer tees.

Do not solder any of the joints in the tees that will join the arbors to each other. Instead, use pliers to slightly crimp the cups with pipes in them on these tees. Then rotate the pipes to temporarily bind the joints together. Solder all other joints.

Construct the Arch

Working on a flat surface, connect two 14¾" lengths of pipe, using a 90° elbow. Add a tee, then a 15" length of pipe to each side. Repeat to form a second, identical arch.

Slide a 45° elbow onto each dowel of the support jig, then slide the legs of the arches onto those elbows.

Add 19½" lengths of pipes between sets of tees, forming horizontal supports as indicated on page 107.

Soldier the arch assembly, except leave the 45 degree elbows unsoldered.

Put the leg assemblies back onto the support jig and fit the arch assembly into place; solder 45-degree elbows to arch and leg assemblies.

Repeat to build as many arbors as necessary.

Install the First Arbor

Use stakes and string to create a straight line for the position of the arbors. Set the arbors in place, 19½" apart and aligned with the string.

Push down on the sides of the first arbor to mark the position of the legs onto the ground; remove the arbor. At two opposite corners, drive a 3-ft. piece of rebar about 18" into the ground.

(Caution: buried utility lines are dangerous. Have your provider mark the utilities before digging any holes or driving anything deep into the soil.)

Fit two legs of the arbor over the buried rebar, firmly anchoring it in place.

Connect the Remaining Arbors

Align second arbor with your string 19½" inches from the first arbor. See "Install the First Arbor" above and anchor the second arbor like the first.

Cut, prep, and fit the horizontal braces between arbors. Keep them all the same length, if they need to vary from 19½".

Solder horizontal braces in tees. Solder leg assembly pipes into the tees at the same time.

Repeat for remaining arbors.

SOLDERING TIP

1. Clean and scour mating surfaces of pipes and fittings with emery cloth or a wire brush.

2. Apply soldering flux to prepared surfaces.

3. Fully insert all pipes that will be joined to a given fitting before soldering that fitting.

4. Unroll 8" of solder and bend the top 2 inches to a 90-degree angle.

5. Put on leather gloves and eye protection. Heat fitting with torch until solder melts when pressed against pipe.

6. Remove torch and press ½ to ¾" of solder into each joint. The solder will move around the joint by capillary action.

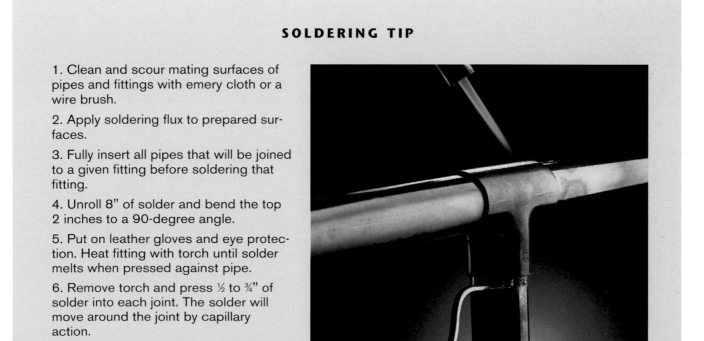

Framed Trellis Wall

This simple design creates a sophisticated trellis wall that would work in many settings. Part of its appeal is that the materials are inexpensive and the construction remarkably simple.

It can be used as a accent wall, a backdrop to a shallow garden bed, or as a screen to block a particular view. As a vertical showcase for foliage or flowers, it can support a wide display of colorful choices. Try perennial vines such as Golden Clematis (*Clematis tangutica*) or Trumpet Creeper (*Campsis radicans*). Or, for spectacular autumn color, plant Boston Ivy (*tricuspidata*). If you prefer annual vines, you might choose Morning Glories (*Ipomoea tricolor*) or a Black-eyed Susan Vine (*Thunbergia alata*). The possibilities go on and on—just make sure that the plants you select are well-suited to the amount of sunlight they'll receive.

Depending on the overall look you want to achieve, you can paint, stain, or seal the wall to contrast with or complement your house or other established structures. Well-chosen deck post finials can also help tie the wall into the look of your landscape.

This project creates three panels. If you adapt it to use a different number of panels, you'll need to revise the materials list.

TOOLS & MATERIALS

- Tools & materials for setting posts
- Tape measure
- Framing square
- Hammer
- Chalk line
- Line level
- Hand saw
- Paintbrush & roller
- Circular saw
- Drill
- Caulk gun
- Nail set
- Pressure-treated, cedar, or redwood lumber:
  - 4 × 4 posts, 10 ft. min. (4)*
  - 1 × 5 posts, 4 ft. (1)
  - 2 × 4s, 10 ft. (3)
  - 1 × 4s, 10 ft. (12)
  - 1 × 1s, 10 ft. (12)

- Paint, stain, or sealer
- 4 × 8-ft. ½ lattice panels (3)**
- 10d corrosion-resistant casing nails
- 4d corrosion-resistant finish nails
- 6d corrosion-resistant finish nails
- Construction adhesive
- Deck post finials (4)
- Speed square
- Combination square
- Folding stick ruler

*We recommend ground contact pressure treated posts set in concrete. KDAT (Kilt Dried After Treatment) if a finish is to be applied. Taller posts may be needed for deep-freezing ground.

**Get pre-finished lattice if possible, or consider renting a sprayer.

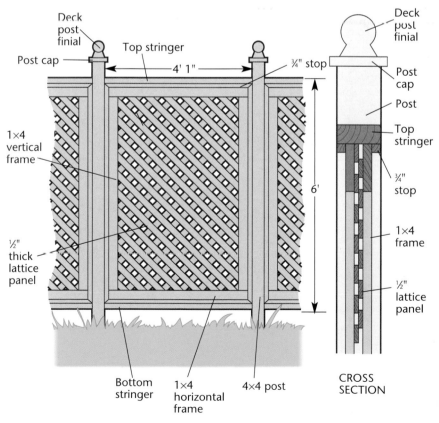

1 Set posts and let concrete cure for two days. Snap a level chalk line to locate top stringers. Trim your posts square six inches above the chalk line.

HOW TO BUILD A FRAMED TRELLIS WALL

Set the Posts

Set the four posts with tops at least 7½ ft. above ground. Dig postholes 52½" apart on-center. Place 4 × 4s in the holes and gap with a spacer bar to ensure 49" face-to-face spacing of posts. For a wall of this height,

Cutting List

Part	Lumber	Size	Number
Posts	4 × 4	10 ft.	4
Stringers	2 × 4	48"	6
Back frame			
Top & bottom		1 × 4	41" 6
Sides	1 × 4	72"	6
Front frame			
Top & bottom		1 × 4	48" 6
Sides	1 × 4	65"	6
Stops			
Top & bottom		1 × 1	48" 12
Sides	1 × 1	70½"	12
Lattice panels	4 × 8	48 × 72"	3
Post caps	1 × 6	4½ × 4½"	4

Deck post finial

Post cap

Top stringer

4' 1"

¾" stop

1×4 vertical frame

½" thick lattice panel

6'

Bottom stringer

1×4 horizontal frame

4×4 post

Deck post finial

Post cap

Post

Top stringer

¾" stop

1×4 frame

½" lattice panel

CROSS SECTION

we recommend setting pressure treated posts in concrete in belled holes. Read "Laying Out a Fenceline" and "Installing Posts" to properly align, plumb, space, and set posts.

On the first post, measure and mark a point 77" from the ground. Using a framing square, draw a level line across the post at the mark. Tack a nail in place along the line, and tie a chalk line to it. Stretch the chalk line to the opposite post, then use a line level to level it. Remove the line level and snap a line across all 4 posts.

Transfer the chalk line to the inside faces of the posts for the upper stringer locations with a combination square. On each post, measure down 72" from the chalk line and transfer this measurement to the inside faces with a square to locate the lower stringers.

Trim the posts six inches above the chalk line using a clamped speed square and a circular saw. Prime, stain or seal the posts.

Prepare Pieces & Position Stringers

Cut and tag the stringers and top and bottom stops to fit precisely between your posts, take separate measurements for bottom and top pieces and individual bays. Note: If top and bottom stringers diverge from each other by more than ½" within a bay, use temporary cross bracing between post tops to bring posts closer to parallel.

Cut top and bottom frame pieces ½" shorter than your stringers. Cut vertical pieces according to cutting list. Prime, stain or seal all pieces. Develop a system for keeping track of their positions in the wall.

Starting with your middle bay, attach your top stringers above the top stringer lines scribed on the posts. Attach your bottom stringers below the bottom stringer lines. This should leave a 49" × 72" opening for the frames. Use 16d H.D. galvanized casing nails to secure stringers. Drill pilot holes as needed. Set heads with a nail set.

Add Stops to the Back of the Fence Frame

Position a 1 × 1 stop flush with the back edge of the stringer and post, as indicated on the cross section on page 111. Drill pilot holes approximately every 8", then drive 6d corrosion-resistant finish nails through the stop and into the fence frame.

Set up the Back Frame

On a level work surface, position the pieces of the back frame to form a 48½" × 71½" rectangle with butted

2 Transfer your stringer lines to facing sides of posts with a square. Install stringers to the middle bay first, aligning top stringer above upper line and bottom stringer below lower line.

3 Add the stops to the back side of the fence frame. Drill pilot holes and nail the stops in place with 6d corrosion-resistant finish nails.

112

joints. Measure the opposite diagonals. Adjust the frame until these measurements are equal, ensuring that the frame is square.

Run a bead of construction adhesive around the center of the back frame. Set the lattice panel in place, making sure it's square and centered in the frame.

Attach the Front Frame

Set the front frame in place, with the joints butted in the opposite direction of those on the back frame. Square the frame, then secure the frame with 4d corrosion-resistant finish nails driven every 6". Sink the nails, using a nail set. Let the adhesive cure, according to manufacturer's directions.

Install the Framed Lattice Panel

Set the panel in place between the center posts, positioned firmly against the stops.

Position 1 × 1 stops around the front edges of the frame. Push the stops in until they hold the panel snugly in place. Drill pilot holes approximately every 6" and drive 6d corrosion-resistant finish nails through the stops and into the fence frame.

Complete the Wall

Complete the remaining panels.

Center and attach post caps with 6d nails, driven where they will be covered by the finials.

Draw diagonal lines from corner to corner of post caps to form Xs. Drill and drive your finial bolt on the X and attach the finials. Apply topcoat of paint, stain, or sealer.

4 Set up the pieces of the back frame, butting the joints. Square the frame, then apply a bead of construction adhesive along the center of the frame. Center the lattice panel on the frame.

5 Set the front frame in place, butting the pieces in the opposite direction of the back frame. Drive 4d corrosion-resistant finish nails every 6" to secure the front frame to the lattice panel and back frame.

6 Set the panel in place between the center pair of posts. Add stops on the front side, then drill pilot holes and nail the stops in place, using 6d corrosion-resistant nails.

7 Install the remaining panels and add post caps to the posts. Add a deck finial to each post.

Mortarless Block Wall

Far from an ordinary concrete block wall, this tile-topped, mortarless block wall offers the advantages of block—affordability and durability—as well as a flair for the dramatic. Color is the magic ingredient that changes everything. We added tint to the surface bonding cement to produce a buttery yellow that contrasts beautifully with the cobalt blue tile. However, you can use any combination that matches or complements your wall's surroundings.

Mortarless block walls are simple to build. You set the first course in mortar on a footing that's twice as wide as the planned wall, and extends 12" beyond each end. You stack the subsequent courses in a running bond pattern.

Use concrete block and mortar rated for outdoor use. The wall gets its strength from a coating of surface bonding cement that's applied to every exposed surface. Tests have shown that the bond created between the blocks is just as strong as traditional block-and-mortar walls.

The wall we have built is 24" tall, using three courses of standard 8 × 8 × 16" concrete blocks and decorative 8 × 12" ceramic tiles for the top cap.

Choose a durable, exterior ceramic tile and use a thin-set exterior tile mortar. Be sure to select an exterior grout as well.

HOW TO BUILD A MORTARLESS BLOCK WALL

Dig Trenches for the Footings

Measure and mark the fence line with batter boards and mason's string. Make the length of your wall a multiple of half a full block length plus a little so you won't have to cut blocks. For example: a standard block is 15⅝. Divide by two and get 7¹³⁄₁₆ add a little and get 7⅞.

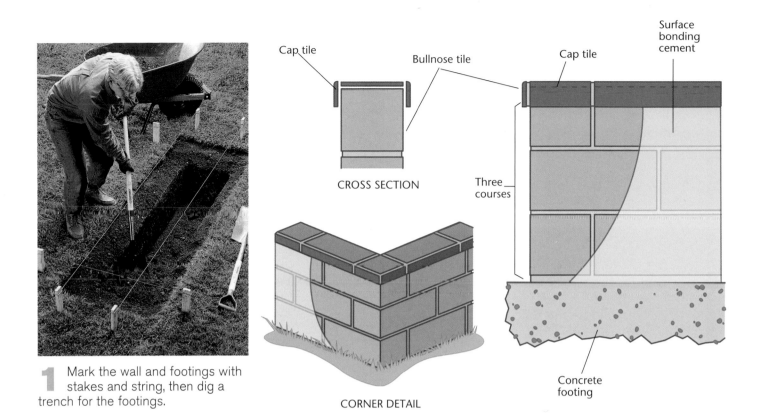

CROSS SECTION

Cap tile

Bullnose tile

CORNER DETAIL

Surface bonding cement

Cap tile

Three courses

Concrete footing

1 Mark the wall and footings with stakes and string, then dig a trench for the footings.

TOOLS & MATERIALS

- Stakes & mason's string
- Hammer
- Line level
- Tape measure
- Shovel
- Wheelbarrow or mixing box
- Hand maul
- Hand tamp
- 4-ft. level
- Hacksaw
- Chalk line
- Circular saw with masonry-cutting blade
- Masonry chisel
- Line blocks

- Mason's trowel
- Notched trowel
- Square-end trowel
- Groover
- Tile cutter
- Caulk gun
- Rubber grout float
- Sponge
- Small paintbrush
- Compactible gravel
- 2 × 4s for footings
- #3 rebar
- 16-gauge wire
- Vegetable oil or release agent
- Cement mix
- Sheet plastic

- Concrete blocks (end, half, & stretcher)
- Type N mortar
- Corrugated metal ties
- Wire mesh
- Surface bonding cement
- Fortified thinset exterior mortar
- 8 × 12" ceramic tile rated for exterior use
- Matching bullnose tile
- Tile spacers
- Sand-mix exterior grout
- Silicone caulk
- Grout sealer

Locate the outside faces of the footings with string and your batter boards. Note that the footings typically extend half the width of your wall block beyond the face and ends of your wall.

Outline your footings. Plan on setting the footing tops at least 4" below the ground, so you may plant over them. Footings for walls meeting at a corner must be square. Dig the trenches, pour the footings and let cure.

Lay Out the First Course of Block

Dry lay the entire first course with the aid of a mason's string and straight edge. Check for square using the 3-4-5 method, and keep the blocks centered on the footer. Use a half-length end block if needed.

If you need to cut a block, score your line with a masonry blade and break the block with a hammer and cold chisel. Put the cut block early in the run, and position the same size cut block in a similar position in subsequent courses to maintain the joint offset.

Set a mason's line ¼" above your blocks and in line with the outside face of the wall.

Mark the position of end and corner blocks on the footing with a pencil, and remove the blocks.

Snap chalk lines to connect the end and corner block marks.

Set the First Course

Mix and pour concrete so it reaches the tops of the forms. Work the concrete with a shovel to remove any air pockets.

Screed the surface of the concrete by dragging a short 2 × 4 along the top of the forms. Add concrete to low areas, and screed again.

When concrete is hard to the touch, cover the footings with plastic and let the concrete cure for 2 to 3

days. Remove the forms and backfill around the edges of the footings. Periodically check to make sure the blocks are plumb, level, and aligned with your string.

Let the footings cure for a week.

Stack Remaining Blocks

Dry-stack successive block courses except for the top course. Keep joints staggered and use half end blocks where needed at wall ends.

Draw a mason's string across corner and end blocks and shim wayward blocks into alignment if necessary. Continually check blocks for plum and level.

Lay wire mesh on top of the second-to-top course. Install the top course.

Fill the block hollows with mortar. Trowel the surface smooth.

Build Up the Corners & Ends

At a corner, begin the second course with a full-sized end block stacked so that it spans the vertical joint where the two runs meet. Make sure the block is level and plumb. If a block requires leveling, cut a piece of corrugated metal tie and slip it underneath. If a block is off by more than ⅛", remove the block, trowel a dab of mortar underneath, and reposition the block.

Butt a full-sized stretcher block against the end block to form the corner. Use a framing square to make sure the corner is square.

Build the corner up three courses high. Keep blocks level and plumb as you go, and check the position with a level laid diagonally across the corners of the blocks.

Build up the ends of the wall three courses high; use half-sized end blocks to offset the joints on the ends of the wall.

TIP: MAKING ISOLATION JOINTS

If your wall abuts another structure, such as the foundation of your house, slip a piece of ½"-thick asphalt-impregnated fiber board into the end of the trench to create an isolation joint between the footing and the structure. Use a few dabs of construction adhesive to hold the fiber board in place.

The fiber board keeps the concrete from bonding with the structure, which allows each to move independently. This minimizes the risk of damage during freeze and thaw cycles.

2 Build 2 × 4 forms and stake them in place. Make rebar grids and put them upright in the trench. Coat the inside edges of the forms with release agent.

3 Fill the forms with concrete, screed the concrete level, then float the surface.

4 Lay out the first course of block, cutting blocks as necessary. Mark the ends and corners, then remove the blocks and snap reference lines.

5 Mist the footing with water, then lay a ⅜"-thick bed of mortar inside the reference lines.

Fill in the Subsequent Courses

Set your mason's string level with the corner and end blocks of the second course.

Fill the second course with stretcher blocks, alternating from the end to the corner until the blocks meet in the middle. Maintain a standard running bond with each block overlapping half of the one beneath it. Trim the last block if necessary, using a circular saw and masonry-cutting blade or a hammer and chisel.

Use a level to check for plumb and line blocks and a line level to check for level. Lay wire mesh on top of the blocks.

Install the top course, then fill block hollows with mortar and trowel the surface smooth.

Apply Surface-bonding Cement

Starting near the top of the wall, mist a 2 × 5-ft. section on one side of the wall with water. (The water keeps the blocks from absorbing all the moisture from the cement once the coating is applied.)

Mix the cement in small batches, according to the manufacturer's instructions, and apply a $\frac{1}{16}$"- to $\frac{1}{8}$"-thick layer to the damp blocks, using a square-end trowel. Spread the cement evenly by angling the trowel slightly and making broad upward strokes.

Use a wet trowel to smooth the surface and to create the texture of your choice. Rinse the trowel

6 Starting at the first corner, stack a full-sized end block so it overlaps the vertical joint at the corner. Build the corners and ends three courses high.

7 Fill in the subsequent courses. On the next to the last course, lay wire mesh over the block, then install the final course. Fill the block hollows with mortar.

8 Apply the surface-bonding cement to damp blocks, using a square-end trowel. Smooth the cement and cut grooves as necessary.

frequently to keep it clean and wet.

To prevent random cracking, use a groover to cut control joints from top to bottom, every 48". Seal the hardened joints with silicone caulk.

Set the Tiles

Lay out the 8 × 12" ceramic tiles along the top of the wall, starting at a corner. If any tiles need to be cut, adjust the layout so that the tiles on the ends of the wall will be the same size.

Apply latex-fortified exterior thinset mortar to the top of the wall, using a notched trowel. Spread the mortar with the straight edge, then create clean ridges with the notched edge. Work on small sections at a time.

Place the corner tile, twist it slightly, and press down firmly to embed it in the mortar. Place each tile in this same manner, using tile spacers to keep the tiles separated.

Lay out the bullnose tile on each side of the wall. Again, start in a corner and make sure that the tiles at the ends of the wall will be the same size. Cut tile as necessary.

Apply mortar to the sides of the wall. Set the bullnose tile in the same way that you set the top tile. Tape the tile in place until the mortar dries.

Remove the spacers and let the mortar cure for at least 24 hours.

Grout the Tile

Mix a batch of sanded grout. NOTE: adding latex-fortified grout additive makes it easier to remove excess grout.

Spread a layer of grout onto a 4- to 5-ft. area of tile. Use a rubber grout float to spread the grout and pack it into the joints between tiles. Use the grout float to scrape off excess grout from the surface of the tile. Scrape diagonally across the joints, holding the float in a near-vertical position.

Use a damp sponge to wipe the grout film from the surface of the tile. Rinse the sponge out frequently with cool water, and be careful not to press down so hard that you disturb the grout.

Continue working along the wall until you've grouted and wiped down all the tile. Let the grout dry several hours, then use a cloth to buff the surface until any remaining grout film is gone.

Apply grout sealer to the grout lines.

9 Lay out the tile along the wall, then set it, using exterior thinset mortar.

10 Grout the joints, using a rubber grout float. Wipe the film from the tile and let it dry. Polish the tile with a soft, dry rag.

Dry Stone Wall

Many homeowners —especially dedicated gardeners— dream of using low stone walls to form the boundaries of their yards or gardens. Sadly, many of them think those stone walls are destined to remain merely dreams. If you're one of those people, you'll be happy to hear that you don't have to hire a mason to build a durable stone wall.

You can construct a low stone wall without mortar, using a centuries-old method known as "dry laying." With this technique, the wall is actually formed by two separate stacks that lean together slightly. The position and weight of the two stacks support each other, forming a single, sturdy wall.

You can construct a low stone wall without a concrete footing and only a little mortar using a centuries-old method known as "dry-laying." The wall is formed by two separate stacks, called wythes, that lean in on each other. When the ground shifts under the wall (as it will), the stones shift with them—there is no monolithic hunk of masonry to crack and crumble because of the movement.

While dry walls are simple, they do require patience and a strong back. Heavy stones must be carefully selected, sorted, and applied in the wall so each course runs level and the wall fits together well. We recommend you use a sedimentary block stone like the limestone we use here. The rectangular shapes and parallel striations make

them natural building blocks. Plus, sedimentary stones are relatively easy to cut and split. We suggest a masonry blade in a circular saw to score the stones if needed and a stone chisel and hand sledge to split them. Please wear eye and ear protection.

For this wall, you'll need stones in four general categories.

- Shaping: half or less as wide as the wall and any length. Sedimentary rock is sold in relatively consistent widths and variable lengths. Longer shaping stones make for a more stable wall.
- Tie: These are stones that are as long as the wall is wide.
- Filler: Also called rubble, these are small and irregular fragments that fit into cracks and fill the spaces between the wythes.
- Cap: These are large, flat stones, sometimes called flags that are wider than the top of your wall.

This kind of wall must be at least half as wide as it is tall, and the wall must have a batter, that is, it must get narrower as it goes up. The wall we build here didn't need much of a batter because of the regularity of the stones, but walls of less even stones need a considerable inward lean to stay standing as the ground shifts during freeze/thaw cycles. This requires spacing the lower wythes farther apart and filling the gap with rubble. We use mortar on the capstones to keep these from being knocked off. Some of these mortar joints will break over time, but this shouldn't compromise the overall strength or beauty of the wall.

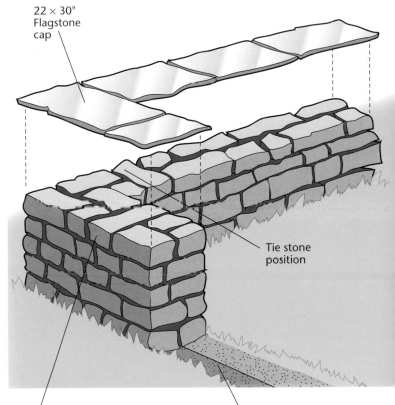

22 × 30" Flagstone cap

Tie stone position

Tie stone position

24" sloped trench for 1st course

HOW TO BUILD A DRY STONE WALL

Dig a Trench

Sort the stones by size and purpose, placing them in piles near the building site.

Measure and mark the outside face of the wall with a mason's string. Walls meeting at a corner may be squared using the 3-4-5 method.

Outline and dig a 24" wide trench within your outside fence line. (You can widen this if you have large stones or need more of a batter). Set a level mason's line above the trench, and keep the bottom of the trench a consistent distance below the line.

1 Dig a trench. As you deepen it, make the sides vertical, but create a V shaped dip in the bottom. Keep the trench a consistent distance below a level mason's line.

2 Set your first course in a bed of un-compacted class V. Tie your corners together. Note: These wide stones spanned the trench. You might have gaps between the wythes of your lower courses, which you'll fill with rubble stonc.

3 Use stone fragments to fill gaps and level your stones. Long stones overlapping at corners help stabilize the wall.

4 Add tie stones every three feet or so on your third course. Continue to level individual stones, and level and align the stones along the length of the wall with a 4' level.

5 Attach the cap stones with mortar, kept back from the face of the wall. Use chips to help level the caps.

Deepen your trench to a minimum of six inches at the sides and 8" inches in the middle. The sides should be vertical. The bottom will assume a gentle, V-shaped furrow. Because you are following a level line, the trench may get deeper in places.

Compact loose soil with a hand tamper. Line the trench with two inches of gravel sub-base, maintaining the V shaped dip in the center and the consistent distance from the level line. **Do not compact the sub-base.**

Build the First Course

Begin laying pairs of shaping stones in two rows along the bottom of the trench. These can be somewhat irregular, wide and short stones. Position them flush with the edge of the trench and sloping toward the center. If you have a corner, start there, meshing the intersecting walls together.

Place the uneven sides of your stones down in the gravel and push or dig them in. We used 12" wide stones for the bottom course, since the wall is wider at the bottom. Your two rows may have a gap in the center, which you need to fill with rubble stone.

Use a bullet level to level individual stones front to back. Individual stones will continue to slant in toward the centerline of the wall. Use a 4' level to keep the stones within a wythe level and to keep the wythes level with each other.

As you approach the end, cut stones as needed, but use long stones for the very end. Cut stones across the "grain" by scoring them with a circular saw with a masonry blade and breaking with a hand sledge and stone chisel. Layered stone may separated along the layers without scoring

Build the Second Course

Use large, long evenly shaped stones at the corners of the second course. Overlap the stones of the meeting walls in a way that ties the walls together.

Work down the line with shaping stones, staggering the joints with the joints of the course below. You may shim and space stones as needed with stone fragments.

Use your bullet level to keep stones level in line with the wall. Side to side the stones continue to slant in. Use your 4' level along the top and sides of shaping stones to keep the wall level and straight.

You may need tie stones across the width of the wall near the corners and ends; otherwise, only use parallel shaping stones on the second course.

Each consecutive wall course should be slightly narrower then the one below, causing the wall faces to slope inward. Use long shaping stones at the end of the wall, cutting the stones preceding those if needed.

Note: We used stones of diminishing breadth toward the top, but you may use stones of a consistent breadth and fill gaps left between wythes with rubble stone.

Finish Laying Wall Blocks

Continue each course, tying corners together with long overlapping stones and using long stones toward the wall ends.

Every third course, use tie stones across the width of the wall to hold the wythes together. Space these every three feet or so.

With each successive course, the wall should become narrower, either by using narrower stones or by reducing the rubble-stone gap between the wythes.

You may mortar in the final course below the capstones or not. Keep mortar well away from the outside face of the wall so it will not show.

Set the Capstones

Apply a stiff mortar to the top blocks far enough from the stone faces that it will be concealed. Level the capstones on the tops. Use slivers of stone for shims.

Clean mortar off the stone faces with a damp rag and a brush before it cures.

VARIATIONS: SLOPES AND CURVES

If the wall goes up- or downhill, step the trench, the courses, and the top of the wall to keep the stones level.

To build a curved wall, lay out the curve using a string staked to a center point, and dig the trench and set stones as for a straight wall.

If slope is an issue along your wall site, you can easily step a dry stone wall to accomodate it. The key is to keep the stones level so they won't shift or slide with the grade, and to keep the first course below ground level. This means digging a stepped trench.

1. Lay out the wall site with stakes and mason's string. Dig a trench 4" to 6" deep along the entire site, including the slope. Mark the slope with stakes at the bottom where it starts, and at the top where it ends.

2. Begin the first course along the straight-line section of the trench, leading up to the start of the slope. At the reference stake, dig into the slope so a pair of shaping stones will sit level with the rest of the wall.

3. To create the first step, excavate a new trench into the slope, so that the bottom is level with the top of the previous course. Dig into the slope the length of one and a half stones. This will allow one pair of stones to be completely below the ground level, and one pair to span the joint where the new trench and the stones in the course below meet.

4. Continue creating steps, until the top of the slope. Make sure each step of the trench section remains level with the course beneath. Then fill the courses, laying stones in the same manner as for a straight-line wall. Build to a maximum height of 36", and finish by stepping the top to match the grade change, or create a level top with the wall running into the slope.

Curved Wall

1. If you'd like a curved wall or wall segment, lay out each curve, as demonstrated on page 20. Then dig the trench same as for a straight wall, sloping the sides into a slight "V" toward the center.

2. Lay the stones as for a straight wall, but use shorter stones; long, horizontal stones do not work as well for a tight curve. Lay the stones so they are tight together, off-setting the joints along the entire stretch. Be careful to keep the stone faces vertical to sustain the curve all the way up the height of the wall.

Mortared Stone Wall

The classic look of a mortared stone wall adds a sense of solidity and permanence to a landscape that nothing else can match. Although building a mortared wall takes more work than building a dry-laid one, in some cases, the tailored look of mortared stone is just what's needed.

Plan and position your wall carefully—making changes requires a sledgehammer and a fair amount of sweat. Before you begin work, check local building codes for regulations regarding the size and depth of the footings as well as construction details. And remember, in most communities any building project that requires a footing requires a building permit.

Plan to make your wall no more than 18" wide. Purchase a generous supply of stone so that you have plenty to choose from as you fit the wall together. Laying stone is much like putting a jigsaw puzzle together, and the pieces must fit well enough that gravity and their weight—rather than the strength of the mortar—will hold the wall together. Your stone supplier can help you calculate the tonnage necessary for your project, but you can make rough estimates with these formulas:

Install the Footings & Dry-Fit the First Course

Measure and mark the fence line with batter boards and mason's string.

Locate the outside faces of the footings with string and your batter boards. Note that the footings typically extend half the width of your wall beyond the face and ends of your wall. Check with your stone yard for local recommendations.

Rough Tonnage Calculations:

Ashlar: the area of the wall face (sq. ft.) divided by 15 equals the number of tons needed.

Rubble: the area of the wall face (sq. ft.) divided by 35 equals the number of tons necessary.

TOOLS & MATERIALS

- Tools & materials for pouring footings
- Stakes & string
- Line level
- Tape measure
- Wheelbarrow or mixing box
- Hand maul
- Masonry chisel
- Chalk
- Mason's trowel
- Batter gauge
- 4-ft. level
- Jointing tool
- Stiff-bristle brush
- Stones of various shapes and sizes
- Type N mortar
- ⅜" Wood shims

Outline your footings. Plan on setting the footing tops at least 4" below the ground, so you may plant over them. Footings for walls meeting at a corner may be squared using the 3-4-5 method. Dig the trenches, pour the footings and let cure.

Sort the stones size and shape along your footer. Set aside stones of the right length as tie stones. Using wider stones, lay out 3-4' of the wall, starting at a corner, integrating the two wall sections, leaving ½ to ¾" between stones end to end. You may leave a gap in the middle of the wall as needed to bring wall to the desired width.

Using stakes, mason's string, and a line level, set up a level string about an inch above your stones in line with the outside face(s) of the wall. Trace the positions of your first stones on the footer with chalk as you remove them, and position them as they were in the wall off the footer.

Lay the First Course

Mix a batch of mortar, following manufacturer's directions. Mist the first 3 to 4 ft. of the footing with water, and then lay a 2"-thick mortar bed on the area.

Working along one side of the first course; set stones into the mortar bed. Wiggle each stone after you set it in place, then use the handle of a trowel to tap it down, just firmly enough to remove any air bubbles from the mortar bed.

Set the other side of the first course in the mortar bed. Fill the center with smaller stones and mortar; leave the center slightly lower than the outer edges. If you need to reposition a stone, wash off the mortar before resetting it.

Working along the string side of the first course, set stones into the mortar bed, tapping and wiggling them down to just below your mason's line, keeping the vertical stone faces approximately in line with the mason's line. If the weight of the stones squeezes out too much mortar, support them with temporary wedges. When the mortar stiffens, you can remove the wedges and replace with mortar.

Set the other side of the first course in its mortar. Tap these stones level with the previously set row of stones using a carpenters level to check. Pack the center and joints between stones with small stones and mortar. Keep mortar about an inch from the face of the stones.

Continue setting 3-4' of stones at a time until you've completed the first course. Cut stones as needed with a baby sledge and stone chisel. If needed, score the stones first with a circular saw equipped with a masonry blade.

Add Successive Courses

Adjust the string and line level to indicate the height of the next course.

Dry-fit the second course, 3 to 4

ft. at a time; add a tie stone at the beginning of each section. Stagger the vertical joints by setting one stone over two and two over one.

Set the stones aside in the layout you have established. Lay a 2" bed of mortar over the first course, then replace the stones. Check the slope with a batter gauge, and use wood shims to support large stones so their weight doesn't displace the mortar. Keep the side relatively plumb, checking with a 4-ft. level.

When the mortar is set enough to resist light finger pressure (about 30 minutes), smooth the joints, using a jointing tool. Keep the mortar 1" back from the faces of the stones. Remove the shims and fill the holes. Remove dry spattered mortar with a dry, stiff-bristle brush.

Add the Capstones

Create a level, 1"-thick mortar bed on top of the wall. Center flat stones over the wall and tap them into the mortar.

Fill the spaces between stones with mortar. Tool the joints when the mortar is dry enough to resist light finger pressure.

Of Interest

Adding points of interest along a fence or wall can change the entire personality of a landscape. Look for ways to incorporate unexpected features.

- Paint a trompe l'oeil mural on a wall. To emphasize the dimensional effect, add plants that seem to extend from the painting.
- Attach eyehooks to a wall and thread rope or wire through them in an irregular pattern. Train vines to grow along the guidewires and keep them trimmed to create a random looking lattice effect.
- Prop a ladder against a fence and arrange potted plants on the steps. Add a few on the ground and several hanging nearby to fill out the scene.
- Espalier a tree against a wall by training its limbs to lie flush against the wall. Fruit trees, such as apple trees, take well to this age-old treatment.

A trompe l'oeil scene (above) surrounded by shutters gives the impression of a view beyond this solid wall.

Imaginative use of rustic materials (right) lends a festive air to this casual courtyard.

- Hang a window sash and a window box along the frame of a fence. Plant the window box with annuals and train vines to grow up and around the window sash.
- Attach a bracket to each post in a fence line. Hang a lantern or covered torch from each bracket. (Never leave candles or torches burning unattended.)
- Use a fence or wall to show off an unusual collection. Paint the background in an intense hue and then display a collection of interesting items, such as colorful miniature chairs, birdhouses, or bird cages.
- Fill sap buckets with annuals and hang them in an interesting pattern. Be sure the buckets have adequate drainage—make holes in them before planting, if necessary. And use light-weight potting soil to lighten the load.
- Secure a Victorian trim bracket to a wall or to fence posts. Suspend a lightweight hanging basket from each bracket.
- Bank container plants into a corner. Start with a small tree and stagger heights and sizes of plants to create a lively display. Or, top a low wall with planter boxes and go crazy with annuals and vines.

Castor bean vines curl up this metal fence (above right). Plants can warm up otherwise stark settings, soften harsh lines, or obscure undesirable views.

Vivid color livens up a plain fence and gate (right). Here, cobalt blue sings in a Southwestern setting.

Gates

Although gates are uncomplicated, we ask a lot of them. These simple structures need to welcome family and invited guests at the same time that they turn away intruders. Successful gates need to operate smoothly and keep their attractive appearance for many years with little maintenance.

A gate's allure and interest depend on its materials, color, and pattern, but its strength and durability depend on its structural design and how well it's built. No book can describe gates for every situation, but once you understand the fundamental elements of building a gate, a world of possibilities opens up. The style of your fence and existing landscape will strongly influence your decisions, but after reading through this chapter, you should be able to build a range of gates—from a dramatic trellis-gate combination to a security-conscious arched gate.

Building a gate offers you the opportunity to stretch your imagination and make use of unexpected materials. For example, copper pipe and plumbing fittings, salvaged metal, and stained glass make quite a splash when recycled into gates.

IN THIS CHAPTER:

Gate Types

The type of gate you build will depend on the purpose you want it to serve. Security gates should be tall, sturdy, and difficult to climb—which generally rules out horizontal siding. Gates in privacy fences typically need tall, closely spaced, solid siding.

As you plan your gate, pay particular attention to the width of the opening. If a gate is too wide, it will sag from the sheer load of its own weight. Typically, 48" is the limit for a hinged, unsupported gate. If your opening is wider than that, use a pair of gates.

Another important issue to consider is which way you want the gate to swing. Spend some time thinking about how the gate will be used, and make sure there will be enough space to maneuver the gate as well as an adequate place to stand while opening and closing it. This is especially important if the gate will be positioned at the top or bottom of a slope or steps.

The next step is to choose hardware for the gate, including hinges and latches. The clearance necessary between the gate and the posts will vary, depending on the hardware you select—check the hardware packages for specific requirements. If you're building a gate to fit an existing opening, adjust the gate's dimensions to allow the required amount of clearance. If you're planning a gate for a proposed fence, plan the placement of the gate posts so there is adequate clearance.

The best frame style for a gate depends on its size and weight. Z-frames are perfect for lightweight gate styles. Perimeter-frames provide support for larger or heavier gates. Both frame styles typically need cross braces to keep the gate square and to prevent sagging.

Basic Gate

The basic gate frame styles—perimeter and Z-frame—can be adapted to a wide variety of gate styles. By varying the shape, size, and spacing of the siding, you can create gates to suit almost any style of fence.

Copper Gate

This elegant gate is ideal when set into a living wall or lightly used entry. The design ingeniously combines copper pipe and plumbing fittings to highlight an accent object. You can seal the copper to maintain its original color, speed up the development of a patina, or leave it to weather naturally on its own.

Chain Link Gate

Durable and secure, chain link gates allow you to gain access to your enclosed yard, kennel, or business.

Arched Gate

Designed to complement a tall fence, this striking gate combines ornamental metal with the cedar. Positioned at eye level, the salvaged metal accent actually enhances the security function of the gate by allowing you to see who's approaching.

Basic Gates

If you understand the basic elements of gate construction, you can build a sturdy gate to suit almost any situation. The gates shown here illustrate the fundamental elements of a well-built gate.

To begin with, adequate distribution of the gate's weight is critical to its operation. Because the posts bear most of a gate's weight, they're set at least 12" deeper than fence posts. Or, depending on building codes in your area, they may need to be set below the frost line in substantial concrete footings.

However they're set, the posts must be plumb. A sagging post can be reinforced by attaching a sag rod at the top of the post and running it diagonally to the lower end of the next post. Tighten the knuckle in the middle until the post is properly aligned. A caster can be used with heavy gates over smooth surfaces to assist with the weight load.

The frame also plays an important part in properly distributing the gate's weight. The two basic gate frames featured here are the foundation for many gate designs. A Z-frame gate is ideal for a light, simple gate. This frame consists of a pair of horizontal braces with a diagonal brace running between them. A perimeter-frame gate is necessary for a heavier or more elaborate gate. It employs a solid, four-cornered frame with a diagonal brace attached at opposite corners.

In both styles, the diagonal brace must run from the bottom of the hinge-side to the top of the latch-side, to provide support and keep the gate square.

Buy your gate hardware before you build your gate, since it will affect the clearance between gate and post. Take the diameter of your gatepost and a drawing of your gate to the store to purchase the correct hardware. The placement and orientation of your gate framing and the width of your posts affect which hinges and latches may be properly secured through the siding and into the gateposts and gate framing.

Z frame

Perimeter frame

1 Make sure the gate posts are plumb, then measure the distance between them and calculate the dimensions of the gate.

HOW TO BUILD A Z-FRAME GATE

Calculate the Width & Cut the Braces

Check both gate posts for plumb using a level. If a post is leaning into the gate opening, bolt a turnbuckle & cable sag rod through the top of the leaning gatepost to the bottom of the first line post and try to pull it into line.

Measure the gate opening. Consult the packaging of your hinge and latch hardware, and subtract the needed clearance from the gate opening to arrive at your gate width. Cut two 2 × 4s to this length for your horizontal braces.

Prime, stain, or seal the lumber for the frame and as well as the siding for the gate and let it dry completely.

Attach the Diagonal Brace

Cut two pieces of scrap 2 × 4 to temporarily space the gate stringers. These should align the top and bottom braces of the gate with the top and bottom stringers of the fence.

On a flat work surface, lay out the frame, placing the temporary supports between the braces. Square the corners of the frame, using a framing square.

Place a 2 × 4 diagonally from one end of the lower brace across to the opposite end of the upper brace. Mark and cut the brace, using a circular saw.

Remove the temporary supports, pre-drill and toenail the diagonal brace into position using 4" deck screws.

2 Place a 2 × 4 diagonally across the temporary frame, from the lower corner of the hinge-side, to the upper latch-side corner, and mark the cutting lines.

133

3 Align the end boards of the siding flush with the edge of the frame and attach with screws. Using spacer, position and attach the remaining siding to the frame.

4 Shim the gate into place. Mark the position of the hardware on the gate and gate posts, drill pilot holes and attach the hardware.

Apply the Siding

Position the frame so the diagonal brace runs from the bottom of the hinge side to the top of the latch side. Rip a spacer to the width of the spaces between your fence boards.

Lay out the boards on your frame, starting flush with one end of the gate stringers and spacing your boards with your spacer. If the last board overhangs the stringer ends, measure the overhang. Rip your starting and ending pickets down by half this overhang.

You may clamp a board ripped to the appropriate width against the bottom brace as a placement guide, then attach your end pickets with 2" deck screws.

Infill the remaining pickets, using your spacer to gap.

Hang the Gate

Check to see that your gate will fit and clear the ground. Trim now if needed. Add the finish coat of paint to your gate.

Position your hinges over the gate framing, aligning the hinge pins. Drill pilot holes and drive the screws.

Shim the gate into position. Err on the side of slightly too high against the latch post, as it will sag a bit with time. Drill and drive one top-hinge screw and one-bottom hinge screw and test the gate.

If you need to reposition the gate on the post, fill the first holes in the post with wood epoxy and drive other screws to position the gate. You can drill and drive near the original holes later, with the hinge in place, after the epoxy has cured.

Add your latch and handle according to manufacturer instructions.

Option: Mark the latch post where the inside of the gate stringers come to rest when the gate is latched. Screw a 1 × 2 (or thicker) stop to the post here to keep your latch from having to stop the gate.

HOW TO BUILD A PERIMETER FRAME GATE

Build the Gate Frame

Determine the gate width, purchase your hardware, and cut the horizontal framing as for a Z-frame gate.

On the fence line, measure the distance from the bottom of the upper stringer, to the top of the lower stringer. Cut two pieces of 2 × 4 to this length for the vertical braces.

Prime, stain or seal the lumber for the gate and siding, then let it dry thoroughly.

Form the frame as shown. The horizontal framing covers the end grain of the vertical members. Square each joint with a framing square before drilling holes and attaching with 3" deck screws.

Attach the Diagonal Brace

Position the frame on a 2 × 4 set on edge, running diagonally from the lower corner of the hinge-side to the opposite latch-side corner. Support the frame with 2 × 4 scraps underneath the opposing corners.

1 Determine the lengths of the horizontal and vertical braces of the frame. Lay out the frame, check it for square, and secure the joints with 2½" corrosion-resistant deck screws.

2 Scribe the opposite corners of the frame on the 2 × 4 diagonal brace. Cut the brace, using a circular saw with the blade adjusted for the appropriate bevel angle. Toenail the brace in place.

Measure the diagonal length of the frame from corner to corner, in both directions. Manipulate the frame until these diagonal lengths match; the frame is now square.

Position your diagonal 2 × 4 on the side of each corner that will give you the least acute cut. Mark.

Transfer the cut marks to a face of the 2 × 4, using a combination square. Transfer the angle to your circular saw with an angle finder before crosscutting.

Pre-drill and toenail the brace into position with 3" deck screws.

Attach the Siding

Position the frame so the diagonal brace runs from the bottom of the hinge side to the top of the latch side. Rip a spacer to the width of the spaces between your fence boards.

Lay out the boards on your frame, starting flush with a vertical frame member and spacing your boards with your spacer. If the last board overhangs the frame, measure the overhang. Rip your starting and ending pickets down by half this overhang.

You may clamp a board ripped to the appropriate width against the bottom brace as a placement guide, then attach your end pickets with 2" deck screws.

Infill the remaining pickets, using your spacer to gap.

3 Secure the first and last siding boards to the frame, after trimming if necessary. Space remaining boards as the fence boards are spaced.

The most important consideration when choosing a chain link gate is that the gate should match the color and style of the chain link fabric in the fence, as with this black-coated chain link.

Chain Link Gates

Chain link fences are usually installed more for practical reasons than for aesthetic ones, and that is reflected in the appearance of both the fencing and the gates. Like their counterpart fencing, chain link gates are very easy to install once you understand how the pieces fit together.

If you are installing a brand new chain link fence, start with the gate if you can. Set the gatepost in a belled concrete footing, making sure it is level and plumb. You can set the fence post at the other side of the gate post at the same, or you may choose to wait until you've hung the gate so you know precisely where to locate the post. Then, once the gate is installed, you can install the chain link fence to go with it (the chapter showing how to install chain link fencing is on pages 72 to 78).

You'll find a fair number of design choices if you buy from a fencing contractor or fencing supplier. The fencing contractor can custom-build a gate if you'd like, too—ask them to show you some samples of their work. If you shop at a large building center, you'll be lucky to find more than a small handful of options.

1 Set fence posts in concrete spaced far enough apart to allow for the width of the gate plus required clearance for the latch. Position the female hinges on the gate frame, as far apart as possible. Secure with nuts and bolts (orient nuts toward the inside of the fence).

2 Set the gate on the ground in the gate opening, next to the gatepost. Mark the positions of the female hinges onto the gate post. Remove the gate and measure up 2" from each hinge mark on the gatepost. Make new reference marks for the male hinges.

3 Secure the bottom male hinge to the gatepost with nuts and bolts. Slide the gate onto the bottom hinge. Then, lock the gate in with the downward facing top hinge.

4 Test the swing of the gate and adjust the hinge locations and orientations, if needed, until the gate operates smoothly and the opposite side of the gate frame is parallel to the other fence post. Tighten the hinge nuts securely.

5 Attach the gate latch to the free side of the gate frame, near the top of the frame. Test to make sure the latch and gate function correctly. If you need to relocate a post because the opening is too large or too small, choose the latch post, not the gate post.

Gate with Stained Glass

This gate design started with a stained glass piece we wanted to showcase and grew from there. We know it's unlikely that you'll find a piece with the same dimensions, so we designed a structure that's easy to adapt. Basically, you need to build the frame, cut an opening, and use angle iron to hold your stained glass in place.

The beauty of this gate lies not only in the particular stain glass you choose to display, but also in the opportunity to make it uniquely your own creation. We've chosen a picket shape that reflects the diamond design in our stained glass piece, but any combination that appeals to you can be made to work.

Although this design includes a catch on the latch side post to keep the gate from swinging through the posts, a stained glass inset may not be a great choice for a gate that will be frequently used by young children. In that case, you could use an acrylic panel that mimics stained glass or showcase a completely different type of accent piece.

TOOLS & MATERIALS

- Tape measure
- Circular saw
- Paintbrush
- Hammer
- Chisel
- Drill
- Screwdriver
- Framing square
- Level
- Paint, stain, or sealer
- Angle irons (8)
- Corrosion-resistant 4d finish nails
- Drill/driver and bits

- Pressure-treated KDAT (Kiln-Dried After Treatment) if you intend to finish right away, cedar, or redwood lumber:
  - ¾" trim 8 ft.
  - 1 × 4s, 6 ft. (10)
  - 2 × 4s, 10 ft. (3)
- 1½" corrosion-resistant deck screws
- 2½" corrosion-resistant deck screws
- Hinge & latch hardware
- 2" and 3" deck screws

HOW TO BUILD A GATE WITH STAINED GLASS

Prepare the Lumber & Build the Frame

Measure the height and width of the gate opening and the spacing of the fence stringers to determine the finished size of your gate and the height of the gate frame. Plan on leaving a ½" gap between gate and post on the hinge side and ½" gap on the latch side or follow recommendations on your gate hardware packaging.

Compare your actual dimensions to those in the cutting list at right and make necessary adjustments. Cut the lumber. Prime, stain, or seal the pieces on all sides and edges.

Lay out the parts of the frame and mark the cutting lines for the half-lap joints (see diagram at right).

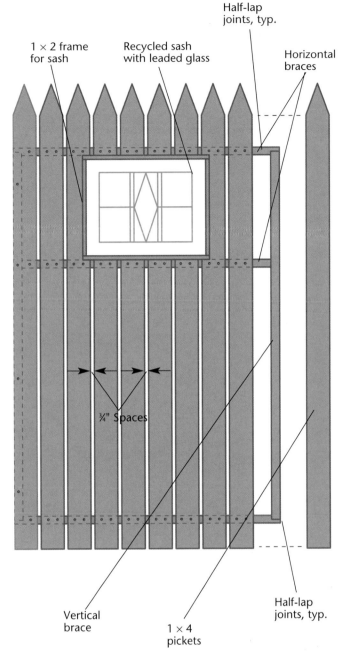

1 Lay out the frame, then mark and cut the lap joints. Hold the corners to a framing square and predrill your screw holes before driving your screws.

Cutting List

Part	Type	Length	Number
Frame			
Horizontal braces	2 × 4	41¾"	2
	2 × 4	38¾"	1
Vertical braces	2 × 4	62½"	2
Trim			
Horizontal	¾"	22"	2
Vertical	¾"	15¾"	2
Siding Slats	1 × 4	72"	10

Diagram labels:
1 × 2 frame for sash · Recycled sash with leaded glass · Half-lap joints, typ. · Horizontal braces · ¾" Spaces · Vertical brace · 1 × 4 pickets · Half-lap joints, typ.

2 Mark the position for the middle brace, then screw it in place, working through the face of the frame and into the brace.

3 Secure the first piece of siding to the frame, aligning it to be flush with the left edge of the frame. Using a spacer, add the remaining siding.

To make a half-lap joint, set the depth of a circular saw to ¾" and cut along a square line 1½" from the end of the horizontal brace; make a cut approximately every ⅛ to ¼", working from the end of the board or joint area back toward that first cut. Remove the waste material and smooth the cut surface, using a hammer and chisel. Repeat with each of the marked joints.

Hold each corner to a framing square and fasten with 2½" deck screws.

Add the Middle Brace

Use the stained glass window as a spacer to position your middle brace. Mark the brace location on the gate frame. Secure the brace with 3" deck screws.

Attach the Siding

Measure the frame diagonally from corner to corner in both directions. If the diagonals do not match, wrack the frame until they do.

Shape the pickets as desired. Mark the picket edges with a V point where they will meet the top edge of the frame. The pickets' position on the gate should follow their position on the fence when the gate is hung.

Attach the first picket flush with the side frame using 2" deck screws every 6". Use an appropriately sized spacer to gap the remaining pickets.

Cut Out the Display Area

From the back of the gate, set the stained glass piece in place within the frame. Measure to make sure the piece is centered within the frame, then

mark the four corners. Remove the stained glass and drill a hole at each mark.

Turn the gate over and draw lines to connect the holes. Use a framing square and tape measure to make sure the lines create an opening that is square and centered within the frame.

Set the depth on a circular saw to ¾" (the thickness of the pickets), and cut along the marked lines. Finish the corner cuts with a hand or jig saw. Remove the siding in the cut-out area.

Note: You may wish to re-enforce the short pickets over the window opening with a 2 × 4 brace, screwed flat to the top horizontal brace.

Install the Display Piece

Put the gate face down on a flat surface and put the window face down in the opening from the back. The front of the window frame will be flush with the face of the gate.

Place an angle iron at each corner between the window frame and the gate frame. Trace the irons and mark the screw hole locations on window and gate.

Remove the window and screw on the angle irons, pre-drilling as needed. Replace the window and screw the angle irons onto the gate frame.

Add Decorative Trim

Set the decorative trim in place, concealing the joints between the pickets and the frame of the stained glass piece. Drill pilot holes and carefully nail the trim in place, using corrosion-resistant finish nails.

4 Position the stained glass piece within the frame and drill holes to mark the corners. Connect the corners and use a circular saw to cut out the opening.

5 Attach angle irons to the display piece; drive screws through the angle iron and into the frame to secure the display piece.

6 Cut trim boards to fit and nail them into position to cover the gaps between the pickets and the display piece.

7 Install the latch hardware on the gate post, then mark the catch positions on the gate; install the catch on the gate siding.

Hang the Gate

Position your hinges over the gate framing, aligning the hinge pins. Drill pilot holes and drive the screws.

Shim the gate into position, distributing the latch- and hinge side gaps as planned. Drill and drive one top-hinge screw and one bottom-hinge screw and test the gate.

If you need to reposition the gate on the post, fill the first holes in the post with epoxy and drive other screws to position the gate, you can drill and drive near the original holes later, with the hinge in place, after the epoxy has cured.

Add your latch according to manufacturer instructions.

Option: Mark the latch post where the inside of the gate frame comes to rest when the gate is latched. Screw a 1 × 2 (or wider) stop to the post here to keep your latch from having to stop the gate.

Copper Gate

This copper gate is an example of how ordinary materials can be used in extraordinary ways. Despite its elegant appearance, the gate actually is nothing more than simple combinations of copper pipe and fittings and a few pieces of inexpensive hardware.

The best setting for this gate is one in which it is largely ornamental. Although it's sturdy and fully operational, it isn't meant to provide security or to handle a constant flow of traffic in and out of your yard. However, set into a living wall or a section of fence where it receives light use, it can provide decades of service.

Copper pipe and fittings are intended to be exposed to water, heat, and cold, so they're entirely suited to outdoor use. The finish can be protected to maintain the bright color or allowed to develop a patina. To maintain the original color, spray the new copper with an acrylic sealer. On the other hand, if you don't want to wait for the patina to develop on its own, rub the finished piece with the cut face of a lemon or a tomato—the acid will speed the chemical process that creates the patina.

We used a copper watering can for an accent piece, but there's really no limit to what you could choose. If an object appeals to you and can be wired or soldered securely into place, you can make it work. You may have to adjust the dimensions of the display frame, but that's a simple matter of making a few calculations before you begin cutting the copper.

TOOLS & MATERIALS

- Tape measure
- Tubing cutter
- Paintbrush
- 4-ft. level
- Reciprocating saw or hand saw
- Locking pliers or pipe wrench
- Drill
- Emery cloth
- Wire pipe&fitting brush
- Flux
- Solder
- Propane torch
- 4 × 4 posts, 8 ft. (2)
- Paint, stain, or sealer
- Tools & materials for setting posts
- Deck post cap & finial
- ¾" copper pipe, 20 ft.
- Copper pipe, 10 ft.
- ⅝ × ¾ × 1 brass flange bearings (3)
- ¾" 90° elbows (10)
- ¾ to ½" reducing tees (12)
- ¾" tees (3)
- Lag screwhinges for chain link fence (2)
- ⅜" flexible copper tubing
- 8-gauge copper wire (about 8")
- Copper watering can
- 16-gauge copper wire (about 24")
- Corrosion-resistant finishing nails

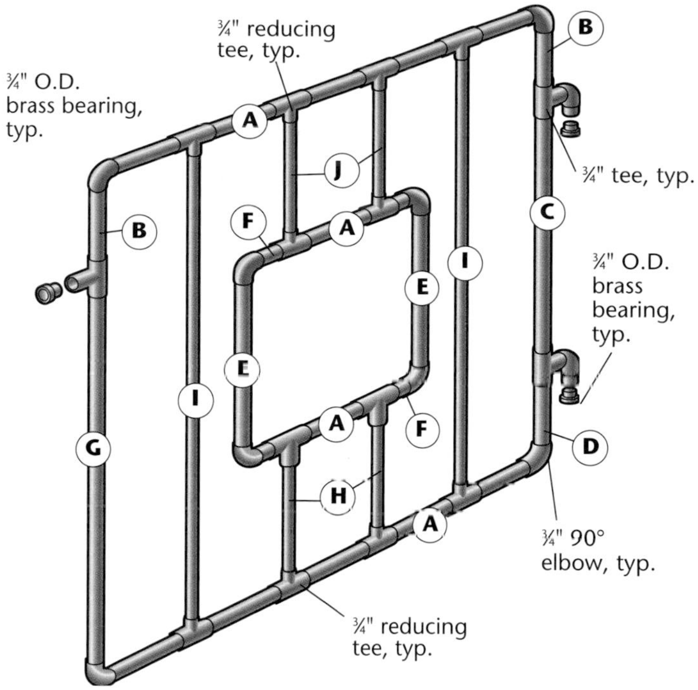

¾" reducing tee, typ.
¾" O.D. brass bearing, typ.
¾" tee, typ.
¾" O.D. brass bearing, typ.
¾" 90° elbow, typ.
¾" reducing tee, typ.
A
B
C
D
E
F
G
H
I
J

CUTTING LIST

Key	Part	Size	Number
A	¾" pipe	6½"	12
B	¾" pipe	6"	2
C	¾" pipe	23¾"	1
D	¾" pipe	5"	1
E	¾" pipe	12½"	2
F	¾" pipe	2½"	4
G	¾" pipe	29½"	1
H	½" pipe	10"	2
I	½" pipe	36¾"	2
J	½" pipe	12¼"	2

HOW TO BUILD A COPPER GATE

Cut the Copper Parts

Measure and mark the pipe, according to the cutting list and diagram at right.

Cut the copper pipe to length, using a tubing cutter. Place the tubing cutter over the pipe, with the cutting wheel centered over the marked line. Tighten the handle until the pipe rests on both rollers. Turn the tubing cutter one rotation to score a continuous line around

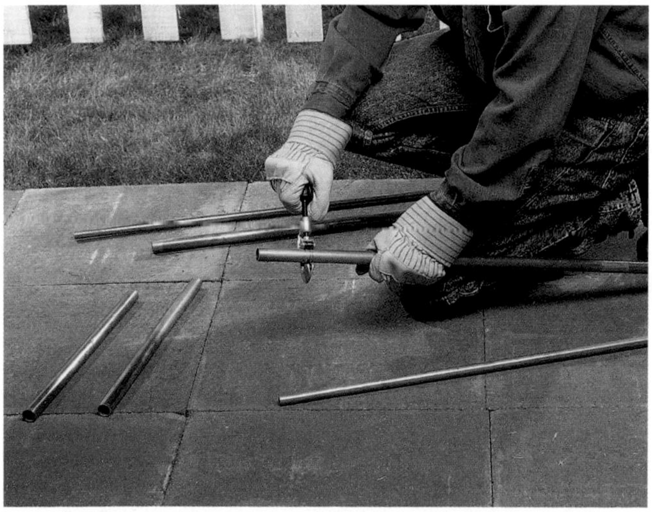

1 Measure, mark, and cut the copper pipe, using a tubing cutter. Clean and flux the pipe and fittings.

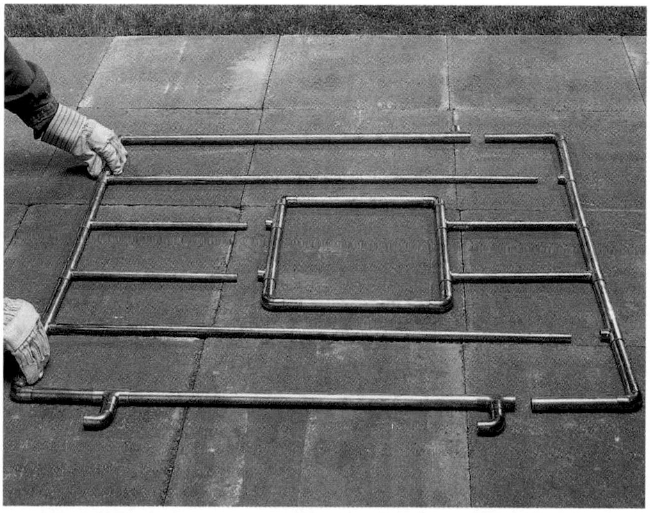

2 Dry-fit the bottom assembly of the gate, and then the top assembly. Connect the two assemblies.

the pipe. Then rotate the cutter in the other direction. After every two rotations, tighten the handle of the cutter. Remove metal burrs from the inside edge of the cut pipe, using the reaming point on the tubing cutter or a round file.

Sand the ends of all the pipes with emery cloth, and scour the insides of the fittings with a wire brush. Apply flux to all the mating surfaces.

Assemble the Gate Pieces

Dry-fit the pieces of the top of the gate and the display frame, referring to the diagram on page 143.

Assemble the bottom run of the gate, again referring to the diagram as necessary.

Join the top and bottom sections of the gate. Measure from one corner of the gate to the diagonally opposite corner. Repeat at the opposite corners. Adjust the pieces until these measurements are equal, which indicates that the gate is square.

Solder the Joints & Add the Bushings

At each of the hinge extensions and at the latch extension, add a brass flange bushing. As you solder these bushings in place, direct the torch's flame more toward the bushing than toward the elbow—brass heats more slowly than copper.

Install & Mark the Gate Posts

Paint, stain, or seal the posts.

Mark the post positions 49½" apart on center. Dig the holes and set the posts. As you plumb the posts, use a 2 × 4 spacer to maintain a 46" distance between the posts top and bottom.

On the first post, measure and mark a point 47½" from the ground. Using a 4-ft. level, draw a line across the post at the mark, then across the opposite post. Trim the posts with a circular saw, using a clamped speed square to guide the cut.

Set a deck post cap and finial on top of each post and nail it in place, using corrosion-resistant finish nails.

Using your trimmed post tops as skids to support your gate, mark the screw hinge location on the hinge

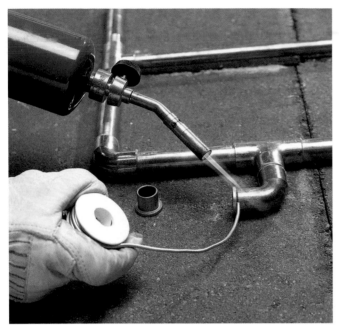

3 Solder the joints of the gate. Add brass bushings to the latch and hinge extensions and solder them in place.

4 Install the gate posts then position the gate and mark the screw hinge locations on the hinge post.

5 Drill pilot holes at the marked locations on the hinge side post. Drive a lag screwhinge into each pilot hole. Make sure the hinge pin is facing up when the screwhinge is in position.

post. Double check that the hinge spacing matches your hinge extension spacing and that the hinge marks are centered and plumb above each other.

Install the Lag Screws for the Hinges

At each of the marked locations on the hinge-side post, drill a ½" pilot hole approximately 2¾" into the post. Drill these holes carefully—they must be as straight as possible.

Drive a lag screwhinge into each pilot hole, using a locking pliers or pipe wrench to twist it into place. The hinge pin needs to be facing up when the lag screw is in its final position.

Test fit your gate. Screw one or the other hinge farther in until the gate hangs level.

Add the Latch

Center a mark on the post for the latch bolt and drill a ⁷⁄₁₆" level hole at that location. (⅜" tubing is ⅜ on the outside)

Cut 15 to 18" of ⅜" flexible copper. Drill a hole through the tubing, 2½" from one end. At the opposite end, form a decorative coil. Cut a 4" piece of #8 copper wire and form a decorative coil at one end.

Insert the latch through the hole in the latch-side post. Thread the wire through the hole in the tubing, then create a small loop below the tubing. This wire loop keeps the latch from falling out of the post.

Hang the Watering Can

Position the watering can within the display frame on the gate. Mark the spots where the handle and spout will meet the copper pipe; clean and flux those areas. Wrap 16-gauge copper wire around the handle of the watering

TIP: SOLDERING COPPER JOINTS

1. To solder, hold the flame tip of a propane torch against the middle of a fitting for 4 to 5 seconds, or until the flux begins to sizzle. Heat the other side of the joint, distributing the heat evenly. Move the flame around the joint in the direction you want the solder to flow.

2. Quickly apply solder along both seams of the fitting, allowing the capillary action to draw the liquefied solder into the fitting. When the joint is filled, solder will begin to form droplets on the bottom of the joint. It typically takes ½" of solder wire to fill a joint in a ½" pipe.

3. Let the joint sit undisturbed until the solder loses its shiny color. When the joint is cool enough to touch, wipe away excess flux and solder, using a clean, dry cloth.

can, using 6 or 8 wraps of wire to connect it to the display frame in the marked spot. Add a little more flux, then solder the handle to the frame. The flux will draw the solder into the crevices between the wire wraps to create a strong, solid joint.

Thread a piece of 16-gauge copper wire through a hole in the spout of the watering can. Wrap the other end of the wire around the display frame in the marked location. Flux and solder the wire wrap as described above.

6 Drill a hole on one end of a piece of flexible copper. At the opposite end, bend a coil. Insert the tubing through a hole in the latch-side post, and thread a loop of wire through the hole in the tubing.

7 Set the watering can into position and secure it, using 16-gauge wire. Solder the wrapped wire to the gate frame.

Arched Gate

With its height and strategically placed opening, this gate is a great choice for maintaining privacy and enhancing security with style. No ordinary "peephole," the decorative wrought iron provides a stunning accent and gives you the opportunity to see who's heading your way or passing by. The arch of the gate also adds contrast to the fence line and draws attention to the entryway.

This gate is best suited to a situation where you can position it over a hard surface, such as a sidewalk or driveway. The combined weight of the lumber and the wrought iron makes for a heavy gate. To avoid sagging and to ease the gate's swing, you'll need to include a wheel on the latch side of the gate. Over a solid surface such as concrete or asphalt, the wheel will help you open and close the gate easily.

Shaping the top of the arch is a simple matter: just enlarge the pattern provided on page 147 and trace it onto the siding. Then cut the shape, using a jig saw.

This piece of wrought iron came from a banister we found at a salvage yard. We used a reciprocating saw with a metal-cutting blade to cut it to a usable size.

TOOLS & MATERIALS

- Tape measure
- Circular saw w/ wood & metal cutting blade
- Paintbrushes & roller
- Hammer
- Chisel
- Drill/driver and bits
- Jig saw
- Level
- Framing square
- Spring clamps
- Caulk gun
- Salvaged piece of ornamental metal
- Pressure-treated KDAT (Kiln Dried After Treatment) , cedar, or redwood lumber:
  - 2 × 4s, 10 ft. (3)
  - 1 × 4s, 8 ft. (13)
- Paint, stain, or sealer
- Posterboard or cardboard
- Construction adhesive
- 1¼" corrosion-resistant deck screws
- 16d nails
- 2" corrosion-resistant deck screws
- 1½" corrosion-resistant mending plates (8)
- 2½" corrosion-resistant bolts and nuts (8)
- Gate wheel
- Hinge & latch hardware
- Gate handle
- Finish nails
- 1½" and 4" deck screws, drop 16d nails

HOW TO BUILD AN ARCHED GATE

Prepare the Lumber

Measure the opening between the gate posts and determine the finished size of your gate. (Check the packaging of your hinge and latch hardware for clearance allowances.) Compare your actual dimensions to those in the diagram below, then check the cutting list and make any necessary adjustments. Cut the lumber for the gate.

Paint, stain, or seal the pieces on all sides and edges. Let them dry thoroughly.

Build the Frame

Lay out the parts of the frame and mark the cutting lines of the half lap joints. If needed, adjust the spacing between your top and middle horizontal braces so the frame of your display piece overlaps the gate framing. To make a half-lap joint, set the depth of a circular saw to ¾" and cut along the marked line; make a cut approximately every ⅛ to ¼", working from the end of the board or joint area back toward that first cut. Remove the waste material and smooth the cut surface, using a hammer and chisel. Repeat with each of the marked joints.

Assemble the frame back side up. Measure diagonally from corner to corner in both directions. When the diagonals match, the frame is square. Secure each lap joint with 1½" screws. (Any points that break through will be concealed by the siding.)

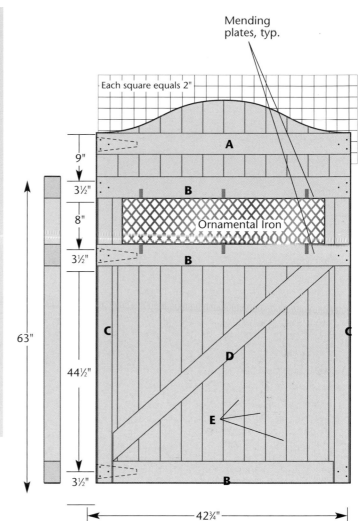

Mending plates, typ.

Each square equals 2"

Ornamental Iron

9"
3½"
8"
3½"
63"
44½"
3½"
42¾"

CUTTING LIST

Key	Part	Type	Size	Number
A	Siding brace	1 × 4	42¾"	1
B	Horizontal braces	2 × 4	42¾"	3
C	Vertical braces	2 × 4	63"	2
D	Diagonal brace	2 × 4	6 ft.	1
E	Siding	1 × 4	8 ft.	12

1 Measure the gate opening and finalize the dimensions of the gate. Cut the pieces, and then paint, stain, or seal the lumber.

Add the Diagonal Brace & Wheel

Check the diagonals again and rack frame into square if needed position a 2 × 4 so that it runs from the bottom of the hinge side of the frame to the first horizontal brace on the latch side. Mark the angle of the cutting lines, then cut the brace to fit, using a circular saw.

Pre-drill and toenail the brace into position using 4" deck screws.

Screw a gate wheel into the vertical support on the latch side of the frame.

Add Siding & Cut the Display Opening

Screw the first and last 1 × 4 siding board in position, flush with the vertical braces and bottom brace. Use three 2" deck screws at each brace. Lay in the remaining boards and space evenly before attaching.

Flip the gate over. Mark a line across the siding, 9" from the top of the frame. Align the top edge of the siding brace along this line, bedding it in construction adhesive. Clamp it in place, flip over the gate, and attach each siding piece to the brace with two 1-1¼" deck screws.

Trace your display piece on the front of the gate, centering it between the top and middle braces (if necessary, drill holes from the back to locate the edges of the framing). Center it side to side as well.

Set the depth on your circular saw to ¾" (the thickness of your siding) and cut along your marked lines. Finish the corners with a jigsaw or hammer and chisel. Remove the cutout siding.

Shape the Top of the Gate

Using the grid method or a photocopier, enlarge the pattern on page 147 and transfer it to a large piece of posterboard or cardboard.

Cut out the shape, then trace it onto the top of the gate. Cut the siding to shape, using a jig saw.

2 Set the blade depth on a circular saw to ¾". Mark the joint, then make a cut every ⅛ to ¼" in the joint area. Remove the waste material, using a hammer and chisel.

3 Position the diagonal brace from the top of the bottom brace on the hinge side to the bottom of the middle brace on the latch side. Mark and cut the brace, and secure with 4" deck screws.

4 Attach the siding with 2" deck screws after spacing the boards evenly. Add the siding brace, then cut out the siding in the display area.

Install the Display Piece

Drill three equally spaced holes across the top and bottom of the wrought iron piece. To drill into wrought iron, start with a small bit and move through increasingly larger bits, drilling slowly and wearing safety goggles.

Set the wrought iron in place and mark corresponding holes onto the horizontal braces at the top and bottom of the cutout. Remove the wrought iron and drill a hole at each mark, drilling all the way through the frame.

Set the wrought iron back into position and line up the holes. For each hole, insert a bolt through a 1½" mending plate, the wrought iron and then the frame. On the back side of the gate, secure the bolts with nuts. Adjust the mending plates so they are square, then mark and drill through the siding and the frame. Install a bolt in each hole, again using nuts to secure the bolts on the back of the gate.

Hang the Gate

Mount the hinges on the gate. Measure and mark the hinge positions. Drill pilot holes and drive screws to secure the hinges to the gate.

Shim the gate into position, leaving requisite space between gate and posts for your gate hardware. If you use a wheel, it should be on the pavement. Plumb the gate with a level. Mark one screw hole on the hinge post for each hinge. Drill and drive these three screws.

Test the gate. If it needs adjustment, fill drilled holes with epoxy and test hang with other holes. When the gate is right, drill and drive remaining holes, but allow epoxy to cure before drilling holes near filled holes.

Install latch and handle hardware according to manufacturer's instructions.

6 Drill holes through the wrought iron and the lumber, then bolt the wrought iron into place.

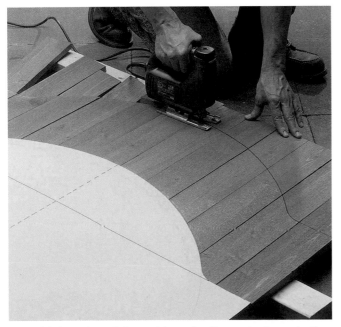

5 Make a template and transfer the arch shape to the siding. Cut along the marked lines, using a jig saw.

7 Mount the hinges on the gate and shim it into position. Fasten the hinges to the post, then install the latch hardware on the gate and post.

Trellis Gate Combination

This trellis gate combination is a grand welcome to any yard. But don't let its ornate appearance fool you—the simple components create an impression far beyond the skills and materials involved in its construction.

This gate is best suited to a location where it will receive plenty of sunlight to ensure an abundant canopy of foliage. It's best to choose perennials rather than annuals, since they will produce more luxurious growth over time. Heirloom roses are a good choice, providing a charming complement to the gate's old-fashioned look and air of elegance.

Larger, traditional styles of hardware that showcase well against the painted wood will also enhance the gate's impressive presentation. The hardware and the millwork that we used are available at most building centers, but you might want to check architectural salvage shops. They may have unique pieces that add another touch of character to the piece.

As with most of our projects, you can alter the dimensions of this project to fit an existing opening. Just recalculate the materials and cutting lists, and make sure you have enough lumber to accommodate the changes.

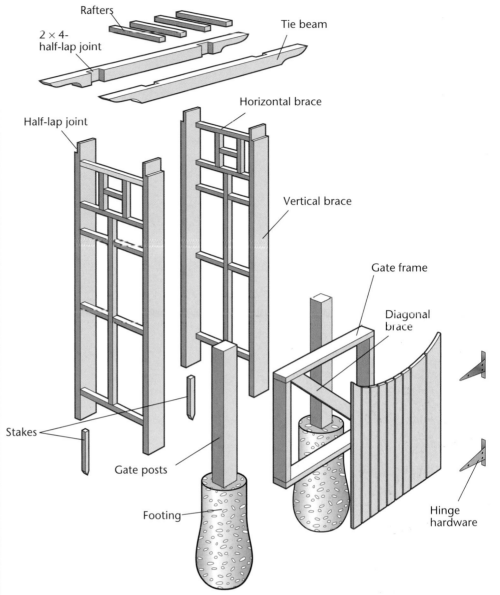

Rafters

2 × 4-half-lap joint

Tie beam

Horizontal brace

Half-lap joint

Vertical brace

Gate frame

Diagonal brace

Stakes

Gate posts

Footing

Hinge hardware

TOOLS & MATERIALS

- Tape measure
- Circular saw
- Paintbrush
- Bar clamps
- Drill
- Carpenter's level
- Framing square
- Jig saw
- Hammer
- Chisel
- Hand maul
- Spring clamps
- Pressure-treated KDAT (Kiln Dried After Treatment), cedar, or redwood lumber:
  - 2 × 2s, 8 ft. (8)
  - 2 × 4s, 8 ft. (9)
  - 1 × 4s, 8 ft. (4)
  - 1 × 6, 8 ft. (1)
  - 1 × 2, 4 ft. (1)
- Paint, stain, or sealer
- 1¼" corrosion-resistant deck screws
- 24" pressure-treated stakes (4)
- 3½" (6 for gate posts) and 2" (4 for stakes)
- 3" and 3½" deck screws
- Cardboard or posterboard
- Sandpaper
- 2½" corrosion-resistant deck screws
- Victorian millwork brackets (4)
- Corrosion-resistant 6d finish nails
- 1½" corrosion-resistant deck screws
- Hinge hardware
- 2" corrosion-resistant deck screws
- Gate handle
- Flexible PVC pipe

Cutting List

Part	Type	Length	Number
Frames			
Horizontal braces	2 × 2	12"	2
	2 × 2	15¾"	8
	2 × 2	33"	6
Vertical braces	2 × 2	17"	4
	2 × 2	54½"	2
	2 × 4	87½"	4
Stop	1 × 2	46½"	1
Top			
Tie beams	2 × 4	72¾"	2
Rafters	2 × 2	33"	4
Gate			
Horizontal braces	2 × 4	40½"	2
Vertical braces	2 × 4	32¾"	2
Diagonal brace	2 × 4	49½"	1
Siding	1 × 4	45¼"	7
	1 × 6	45¼"	2

1 Cut and lay out the pieces for each side of the trellis frame, then secure each joint with 2½" galvanized deck screws.

HOW TO BUILD A TRELLIS GATE

Assemble the Trellis Frames

Measure the gate opening, fence height and fence stringer spacing to size your gate & gate frame. Make necessary adjustments to cutting list on page 151. Cut the lumber, except wait to cut and notch the tie beams until you're ready to measure and install them.

Prime, stain, or seal the pieces on all sides and edges. Let them dry thoroughly.

Lay out one side of the trellis, following the diagram on page 147. Mark the cutting lines for the lap joints and cut the joints, then set the frame back together. Secure the joints with 3" deck screws, pre-drilling as needed. If needed, secure 2 × 2s with finish nails prior to drilling and driving the deck screws.

Repeat to build the remaining trellis frame.

Anchor the Frame to the Gate Posts

Set one of the trellis frames into position with the 2 × 4 vertical brace flush with the fence post edge. If the post is not plumb and cannot be made so, plumb the trellis in the fence line and mark its (slightly canted) position on the fence post. Pre-drill and bolt the trellis to the fence with three 3½" lag bolts.

Attach the second frame in the same manner. Then square both sides by making the diagonal distances between each post and its opposite free trellis brace equal.

2 Position the trellis frames, clamping them against the gate posts. Attach the frame to the posts with 3" lag screws.

3 Square the trellis frames, then secure the free end of each frame to stakes using 3" lag bolts.

Repeat #1 and #2 to attach the other trellis frame to the opposite post.

Secure the Free Sides of the Frames

Drive 24" pressure-treated stakes into the ground flush with the free trellis braces. Recheck your diagonals and mark the trellis brace along an edge of each stake to record correct alignment.

Adjust the frames to level, digging the free braces into the ground or clamping them above ground against the stakes as needed.

With the frames squared and leveled, pre-drill and attach stakes to frames with appropriately sized lag bolts.

Install the Tie Beams

Using the grid method or a photocopier, enlarge the pattern at right, and transfer it to a large piece of cardboard. Cut out the pattern, then trace the shape onto the ends of each 2 × 4 tie beam.

Cut the tie beams to shape with a jigsaw. Clamp the beams in position with the trellis frames held plum and trace the lap joints onto the beams. Cut the lap joints. Prime, stain or seal the cut wood when the joints fit and let dry.

Clamp, drill and fasten the tie beams with five 1½" deck screws per joint.

```
—12"—  ┣3¼"┫  ┣——Variable——┫  ┣3½"┫ —12"—
                      3½"
Each square = 4"
```

Attach the Rafters

Evenly space the four rafters flush with the tops of the tie beams. Pre-drill and attach with 3" deck screws.

Add the Trim

Set a millwork bracket into place at each of the corners between the tie beams and the trellis frame posts. Drill pilot holes and secure the brackets, using finish nails.

Build the Gate Frame

Lay out and screw together gate frame perimeter. Cover the end grain of vertical members with horizontal members. Hold corners to a framing square, pre-drill, and fasten with 3" deck screws. Measure the diagonals of the frame. If they are not equal, rack the frame until they are.

Position a 2 × 4 under the frame so it runs from the bottom of the hinge side to the top of the latch side (see picture). Mark and cut 2 × 4 to fit with a circular

4 Cut 2 × 4s, using the grid pattern, for tie beams. Dado each to accommodate the trellis frame post tops, then clamp into position and attach with five 1½" galvanized deck screws at each joint.

5 Attach four evenly spaced 2 × 2s between the tie beams for rafters, using 2½" galvanized deck screws.

saw. Predrill and attach diagonal through top and bottom perimeter frame with 3½" deck screws.

Add the Siding

Clamp a 2 × 4 across the bottom of the frame to act as a reference for the length of the pickets. Position the siding flush with the lower edge of the clamped 2 × 4.

Test space your boards, keeping the edge boards flush with the edges of the frame. Our gate accommodated two consecutive 1 × 6s on the hinge side followed by seven 1 × 4s, using a ⅝" plywood spacer to gap the boards.

Attach gapped and aligned boards with 2" deck screws. Apply finish coat of paint to trellis and gate if called for.

Hang the Gate

Position the screw holes of the gate-side hinge leaves over gate framing and align hinge pins. Mark hole locations, drill pilot holes and screw the hinge to the gate.

Shim the gate into position. Drill and drive one top-hinge screw and one bottom-hinge screw and test the gate.

If you need to reposition the gate on the post, fill the first holes in the post with epoxy and use other hinge

6 Add millwork brackets at each corner where the tie beams and the trellis frame posts meet. Secure with finish nails.

7 Lay out the gate frame pieces, check for square, and secure the joints with 2½" corrosion-resistant deck screws. Mark and cut the brace, then screw it in place, using 2½" corrosion-resistant deck screws.

8 Clamp a 2 × 4 across the bottom of the gate frame as a guide, then attach the siding. Begin with two 1 × 6s on the hinge side, then finish with 1 × 4s. Use scraps of ⅝" plywood as spacers.

holes to position the gate, you can drill and drive near the original holes later, with the hinge in place, after the epoxy has cured.

Add your latch and handle according to manufacturer instructions.

Option: Mark the trellis frame where the inside of the gate frame come to rest when the gate is latched. Screw a 1 × 2 (or thicker) stop to the post here to keep your latch from having to stop the gate.

Shape the Siding & Add the Gate Handle

Cut a piece of flexible PVC pipe 52½" long (or 12" longer than the width of your gate). Clamp the PVC at the top of the outside edges of the last piece of siding on each side of the gate.

Tack a nail just above the first horizontal brace of the frame at the center of the gate. If this happens to be between two pieces of siding, set a scrap behind the siding to hold the nail. Adjust the PVC until it fits just below the nail and creates a pleasing curve.

Trace the curve of the PVC onto the face of the siding. Remove the pipe and cut along the marked line, using a jig saw. Sand the tops of the siding and repair the finish as necessary.

Attach latch and handle according to manufacturer instructions.

9 Clamp a 1 × 2 to the latch-side gate post and secure with 1½" corrosion-resistant deck screws.

10 Clamp the ends of a length of PVC pipe at each end of the gate top. Deflect the pipe down to create the curve, and trace. Cut to shape, using a jig saw.

Contributors & Credits

MATERIALS CONTRIBUTORS

Midwest Fence
St. Paul, MN
651-451-2221
www.midwestfence.com

CertainTeed EverNew
800-233-8990
www.certainteed.com

Minnesota Vinyl & Aluminum
Shakopee, MN
952-403-0805
www.mvas.com

Trex Seclusions ™ Composite Fencing:
1-800- BUY-TREX
www.trex.com

PHOTOGRAPHY CREDITS

Anchor Wall Systems
Page 96
877-295-5415
www.anchorwall.com

California Redwood Association
Pages 14, 32, 33 (center left), 40
415-382-0662
www.calredwood.com

CertainTeed EverNew
Pages 11 (top left), 59 (top)
800-233-8990
www.certainteed.com

©Walter Chandoha
Page 50

© Crandall & Crandall
page 10 (top), 11 (top right), 123 (both), 124

©Bob Firth/ Firth Photo Bank
Pages 30-31

© Saxon Holt Photography/photobotanic.com
Pages 127 (top), 130, 132, 150

© Charles Mann
Pages 10 (bottom left), 36, 74, 98, 126 (both), 127 (bottom)

Master-Halco
Pages 33 (bottom left), 70
562-684-5066
www.mhfence.com

© Jerry Pavia
page 10 (center), 118 (top left), 131 (top left)

Trex Seclusions ™ Composite Fencing:
Pages 33 (center right), 58, 59 (bottom),
64-65 (all), 66 (top right and center),
67 (top), 68 (bottom right), 69 (bottom)
1-800- BUY-TREX
www.trex.com

Walpole Woodworkers
Pages 4-5, 6-7, 131 (bottom left), 136, Cover
800-343-6948
www.walpole.com

Index

Index (continued)

CREATIVE PUBLISHING INTERNATIONAL

Complete Guide to Bathrooms
Complete Guide to Ceramic & Stone Tile
Complete Guide to Creative Landscapes
Complete Guide to Decks
Complete Guide to Easy Woodworking Projects
Complete Guide to Flooring
Complete Guide to Home Carpentry
Complete Guide to Home Masonry
Complete Guide to Home Plumbing
Complete Guide to Home Wiring
Complete Guide to Kitchens
Complete Guide to Landscape Construction
Complete Guide to Outdoor Wood Projects
Complete Guide to Painting & Decorating
Complete Guide to Roofing & Siding
Complete Guide to Trim & Finish Carpentry
Complete Guide to Windows & Doors
Complete Guide to Wood Storage Projects
Complete Guide to Yard & Garden Features
Complete Outdoor Builder
Complete Photo Guide to Home Repair
Complete Photo Guide to Home Improvement

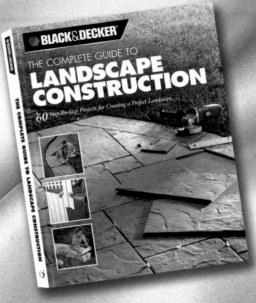

ISBN 1-58923-245-3

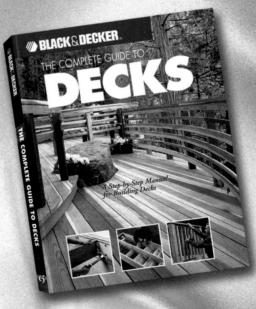

ISBN 1-58923-200-3

CREATIVE PUBLISHING INTERNATIONAL
18705 Lake Drive East
Chanhassen, MN 55317
WWW.CREATIVEPUB.COM